THE COMPLETE GUIDE TO
NORTH AMERICAN
· GARDENS ·

VOLUME TWO

THE WEST COAST

THE COMPLETE GUIDE TO
NORTH AMERICAN
· GARDENS ·

VOLUME TWO
THE WEST COAST

WILLIAM C. MULLIGAN

FOREWORD BY LINDA YANG

Little, Brown and Company

Boston · Toronto · London

First Edition

THE COMPLETE GUIDE TO NORTH AMERICAN GARDENS
was conceived and produced by
Running Heads Incorporated
55 West 21 Street
New York, NY 10010

Editor: Charles A. de Kay
Designer: Liz Trovato
Managing Editor: Lindsey Crittenden
Production Manager: Linda Winters
Photo Editor: Ellie Watson
Photo Researcher: Tonia Smith

ISBN 0-316-58909-8
Library of Congress Catalog Card Number: 90-52884
Library of Congress Cataloging-in-Publication information is available.

10 9 8 7 6 5 4 3 2 1

Published simultaneously in Canada by Little, Brown & Company (Canada) Limited

The photograph of Ohme Gardens on page 14 is reproduced courtesy of Gordon Ohme.

Typeset by Trufont Typographers, Inc.
Color separations by Hong Kong Scanner Craft Company Ltd.
Printed and bound in Singapore by Tien Wah Press (Pte.) Ltd.

ACKNOWLEDGMENTS

The comprehensive nature of this book is such that its development was in no way a single-handed endeavor. For its ultimate realization against sometimes daunting odds, I am enormously indebted to the Brooklyn Botanic Garden's Director Emeritus Elizabeth Scholtz and its Director of Publications Barbara Pesch, both of whom steered me in the right direction, lent encouragement when it was needed and alerted me to worthy gardens I might otherwise have overlooked. In this same regard, heartfelt thanks go to Elvin McDonald, Ann Lovejoy, Jerry Sedenko, Bob Lilly, Lynden Miller, Dr. Stephen Tim, Jacqueline Heriteau, Ken Druse, Sue Lathrop of The American Association of Botanic Gardens and Arboreta, and Linda Yang, whose foreword to this book and positive response to the manuscript at an early stage lifted my spirits immeasurably.

I thank all of the gardens contained herein for their enthusiastic cooperation in supplying information, materials, and photography, and I thank the late David Jacobson, my computer mentor, without whose encouragement and inspiration I never would have become "computerized," and would probably still be hacking away at an antiquated typewriter, much to the dismay of my editor. And he, Charles de Kay, deserves one of the biggest thanks of all for his limitless patience and valuable guidance.

Hugs, kisses, and thanks go to my friends and family members, without whose loyal encouragement and unfailing help in so many ways, this book would never have been written: Eleanor Mulligan, Pamala Hall, Dennis Hall, Carla Glasser, Lawrence Power, Lea Davies, Bonny and David Martin, Hope Hendler, Diane McMullen, Marie Iervolino, Rose and Joseph Kaht, Annette Perazzo, Linda Fox, and Janis Blackschleger.

CONTENTS

FOREWORD

It seems a millennium since that day in the early 1970s when a freckle-faced redhead named Bill Mulligan first came to poke around my city garden and discuss Serious Horticultural Subjects such as how I coped with aphids on my roses in a tiny plot in New York City.

At the time, Bill had already chosen to forgo his original career as a concert pianist, and with several garden articles to his credit, was working as co-editor of a gardening magazine. I was duly impressed with his deft queries, which I have since come to realize were merely his normal work-ing style: a combination of careful study, research, lots of checking, and then lots more checking, again.

And indeed it is his track record of perseverance and careful journalism that leads me to believe that this series of garden guides will provide precisely the beacon that every weary traveler needs.

The idea of trekking through North American public gardens—which includes assorted former private estates as well as arboretums and botani-cal gardens—is a relatively recent phenomenon. Unlike the British, we have no history of national "open-today" gardens. Neither can we boast sites as ancient as Hadrian's estate near Rome, which dates from 138 A.D., or vistas as grand as Le Nôtre's mile-long perspective at Versailles.

But in this vast space between the Atlantic and Pacific we are blessed with a diversity of climate, topography, and soil, and just enough centuries of horticultural influences to have inspired a certain independence—some might even say eccentricity—of landscape thought and design.

It no longer surprises to hear that Americans have an increased interest in gardening. Even the most casual of green thumbs now studies those perfectly pruned and groomed plants in public landscapes with an occa-sional twinge of envy. Indeed it is quickly becoming routine to leave our own weeding and watering chores behind and submit to miles of detours (whether by air, land, or sea) for the pure exhilaration of strolling past intoxicatingly fragrant herbs, exploring woodsy trails edged with unfamil-iar wildflowers, or standing in mute deference before an ancient bonsai.

Which still leaves the problem of unearthing these horticultural gems in the first place. For they are just as likely to be hidden within a Massa-chusetts suburb (such as that which surrounds the Garden in the Woods) as tucked into a mountain-rimmed Pacific peninsula (the breathtaking backdrop for the Botanical Garden of the University of British Columbia).

Helpful garden guides abound on other sides of the seas, but New World explorers have largely been forced to make do with tour books geared to general consumption—wherein is found little solace for the horticulturally inclined. To the rescue at last come these handsome guides, which are also conveniently sized not only for zipping in and out of underseat luggage but for tossing onto a dashboard.

The books are organized into two major sections. The first, which is comfortably readable without distractions, begins by setting the scene with state maps for quick pinpointing of each garden's place. This is followed by Bill's concise essays of that area's significant sites.

Highlighted in these hundred or so compositions is a personal, somewhat eclectic, assortment of subjects, chosen for what Bill believed would be each garden's primary interest to visitors. You feel he's right there, beside you, providing gentle guidance. In addition to the one or more specialized plant collections of note, other particulars range from aspects of the garden's history, its outstanding architectural features, design or stylistic influences, the primary season of interest, and portraits of founders, former owners, or present supporters.

The essays, along with the color photographs, are a superb introduction to these gardens and invaluable not only for excursion plotting and planning but for sedentary armchair dreams.

The latter portion of the book neatly enumerates the nitty-gritty facts. Here are all the essentials required for visiting each place, with directions, addresses, phone numbers, hours, and admission policies. This host of indispensables in capsule form also includes information on varied related activities such as workshops, children's attractions, and library use. Included are symbols delineating the existence of plant labels, guided tours, visitor centers, gift shops, and courses.

Despite the plethora of information these books contain, the perceptive reader sooner or later will note Bill's distinctly nonjudgmental mien—an approach for which I, for one, am grateful. Notwithstanding most gardeners' predilection for voicing strong personal opinions, it is only misleading to attempt to compare a continent of landscapes whose scope encompasses the moody and mysterious as well as the fastidiously restored. It is patently unfair, if not downright impossible, to pronounce equivalents between, for example, the nineteenth-century specimen trees on an elegant former estate (like the Morris Arboretum of the University of Pennsylvania) and the merry kaleidoscope of bedding species (found at Butchart Gardens in Victoria, on Canada's westernmost coast).

On the other hand, it is only natural, if after surveying these glorious gardens, you find yourself trying to determine which, in fact, is Bill's preferred place to linger. Or maybe mine.

However, you're going to have to pick a favorite spot for yourself. Because I'll never tell. And—being a proper reporter—neither will he.

—Linda Yang
New York City

INTRODUCTION

It was my objective in preparing this book not only to illuminate beautiful gardens and to encourage interested travelers to experience their enchanting color and fragrance firsthand, but also to make the reader aware of the increasingly important role these institutions play with regard to ecological and environmental concerns and conservation of endangered species. Information, advice, encouragement, and a sympathetic ear are waiting at many of them for anyone willing to seek them out. At a time of critical threat to the world's ecosystems and overall health of the planet itself, the significance of these organizations grows by leaps and bounds. Their efforts deserve support, and the majority invite membership, for which privileges are granted in return.

The histories of these gardens reflect the history of America itself, its hopes, its dreams, its moral responsibility. Whether a research facility, a university-associated arboretum, an amusement park, a restored private estate, a community park, or a scientifically oriented botanic garden, each invariably represents the passion and vision of a single individual or group determined to create something beautiful and to improve our world in the process.

Read as a whole, this work will reveal certain trends, personal pursuits, and changes in our society. It also supplies much in the way of gardening information and inspiration. But it is still a travel guide, arranged for convenient reference. All of the gardens are listed alphabetically by state and city. The front of the book offers descriptive essays and color photographs of the gardens, while the back contains ready-reference, essential information regarding addresses and telephone numbers, travel directions, hours open, admission-fee policies, degrees of wheelchair accessibility, and special features, such as zoos or museums. Symbols, with a key to their meanings, indicate the presence at each garden of such amenities as a gift shop, plant labeling, a restaurant, parking areas, and availability of courses and membership.

Armchair ruminations are fine. Inspiration from the printed word and the beauty of a well-taken picture are always welcome. But travel the highways and byways and experience nature's boundless beauty and mystery for yourself. There is no substitute.

—William C. Mulligan
New York City

THE
UNITED
STATES

ALASKA

● PALMER

★ JUNEAU

THE GARDENS AT THE MUSEUM OF ALASKA TRANSPORTATION AND INDUSTRY
Palmer

Begun in 1967 in conjunction with the Alaska Purchase Centennial celebration, this museum in the Matanuska Valley contains a fascinating collection of vehicles of all types and periods, from railroad cars and farm machinery to boats and airplanes. Belying the suspicion that the extreme northern environment is too severe to sustain gardens of any kind, the grounds of the museum feature flower beds sparked with cosmos, poppies, spiky snapdragons, mitricaria, pansies, calendulas, lobelias, salvias, alyssum, all kinds of herbs, and, of course, forget-me-nots, Alaska's state flower. There is even a vegetable garden chock full of potato plants and leafy edibles.

Midsummer is the time to visit this spot because this is when everything blooms, even varieties that would normally flower earlier or later in more southern climes. A state Agricultural Experiment Station displaying perennials, annuals, and vegetables is also located in the area, about seven miles southwest of Palmer.

Pansies join the summer bloom festival at Palmer's transportation museum.

CALIFORNIA

FORT BRAGG

DAVIS
SACRAMENTO
FORT ROSS
PLACERVILLE
ROSS
BERKELEY
MILL VALLEY
OAKLAND
SAN FRANCISCO
SAN JOSE
SAN MATEO
SARATOGA
WOODSIDE
SANTA CRUZ
PALO ALTO
SAN SIMEON

PALM SPRINGS
PALM DESERT

SOUTHERN CALIFORNIA

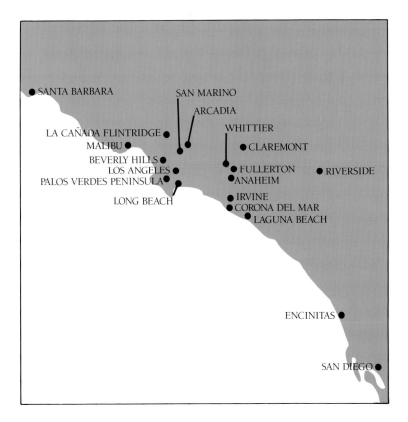

SANTA BARBARA

SAN MARINO

ARCADIA

LA CAÑADA FLINTRIDGE

WHITTIER

MALIBU

CLAREMONT

BEVERLY HILLS

LOS ANGELES

FULLERTON

RIVERSIDE

PALOS VERDES PENINSULA

ANAHEIM

LONG BEACH

IRVINE

CORONA DEL MAR

LAGUNA BEACH

ENCINITAS

SAN DIEGO

DISNEYLAND
Anaheim

In addition to being a kaleidoscope of rides and amusements for children of all ages, Disneyland happens to be a wonderful source of inspiration for gardeners. Ever since the theme park opened in 1955, it has been committed to a philosophy of horticultural integrity, with constantly changing plantings flawlessly installed and scrupulously maintained.

Occasional visits over the years have afforded me the opportunity to watch the park's gardens evolve. During a recent encounter, I was pleased to see how the years have matured the permanent plantings—the bamboos and palms of Jungle World and the shade trees of Main Street, for example—lending many of the exhibits the illusion of authenticity and reality they never quite achieved before.

Of special mention are the fantastical yew topiary animals and geometric forms of every variety that grace the facade of It's a Small World. Sporting the benefits of long-term growth and laborious pruning, they surely represent one of the finest collections of living topiary in America.

For the Victorian-style beds that depict images and spell out words, the annuals and groundcovers, the rock gardens, the seating areas shaded with arbor-trained bougainvillea and mandevilla, the cacti and succulent garden in Frontierland, and the remainder of Disneyland's horticultural delights, we can thank Bill Evans. He is the man who initiated and designed these gardens, as well as those at Disney World Resort in Florida, Tokyo Disneyland, and Euro Disney.

Disneyland's It's a Small World boasts a remarkable display of topiary art.

Sweet garlic (Tulbaghia fragrans) *at LASC Arboretum in late summer.*

LOS ANGELES STATE AND COUNTY ARBORETUM
Arcadia

The mild Southern California climate nurtures a year-round display of color at this 127-acre garden at the base of the San Gabriel Mountains. Informal landscaping harmoniously combines trees, shrubs, rare and exotic plants from around the world with waterfalls, streams, and ponds. Regal peacocks and other exotic birds parading at will complete the peaceable-kingdom ambience. The grounds' highlights include the Aquatic Garden, Meadowbrook, Demonstration Home Gardens, Tropical Greenhouse, Prehistoric Gardens, and Jungle Gardens.

Comprising 4,000 species and varieties of plants arranged according to geographic origins, the arboretum's major collections include: orchids, one of the largest displays in the country, with 10,000 species and hybrids represented; eucalyptus, one of the broadest samplings outside Australia, 150 species; 175 species of prehistoric cycads; 17 varieties of magnolias; 24 species of bottlebrushes (callistemon), flowering shrubs from Australia; 79 species of ficus; 27 species of coral trees (erythrina), the official tree of the city of Los Angeles; and trumpet trees (tabebuia), with clusters of yellow or lavender flowers.

The grounds encompass a variety of historic trees and structures that survive from the nineteenth century to proffer a glimpse of early California life. Numbered among the aged arboreals are a pomegranate (ca. 1840), a ginkgo (ca. 1875), an English oak (ca. 1875), and a Mexican fan palm (ca.

1880), at 125 feet probably the tallest palm in the continental U.S. Designated as California Historic Landmarks are the delightfully gingerbreaded Queen Anne Cottage (1884) and the Hugo Reid Adobe (1839). The Coach Barn (1879) and the Santa Anita Depot (1890) are further remnants of California Victoriana. The Shakespeare Garden; the Herb Garden, with 450 kinds arranged in a formal plan; and Braille Terrace, with aromatics in raised beds and labelled in braille, are more of the grounds' outstanding attractions.

Also containing a plant-science library and an herbarium (a collection of preserved plant specimens), the arboretum began its life in 1947 when the State of California purchased 111 acres of land from Harry Chandler. Further acreage, purchased from the Arcadia Turf Club, was added in subsequent years, and in 1953 the Los Angeles County Department of Arboreta and Botanic Gardens was established to develop and maintain the arboretum. Owned by the State of California and leased to the county, the facility opened to the public in 1955.

BERKELEY ROSE GARDEN
Berkeley

Created by the WPA during the throes of the Depression, this elegantly conceived garden features a 200-foot-long curving pergola crowning the top of tiers of terraces. With roses planted on the terraces and climbing the pergola, the garden forms a spectacular half-circle bank of bloom facing the bay and the San Francisco skyline in the distance. The more than 4,000 bushes assembled represent the newest introductions, plus hundreds of other varieties. Nearby Codornices Park offers picnic areas and woodland-investigating nature trails.

Announcing over 4,000 bushes and climbers with a view of San Francisco.

BLAKE GARDEN
Berkeley

Sitting on a bluff with spectacular views of the Golden Gate Bridge in the distance, is a Spanish-Moorish house designed by Walter Bliss and built for Mr. and Mrs. Anson Stiles Blake in 1924. Mr. Blake was chairman of the University of California's Advisory Board, as well as an expert in California history, and Mrs. Blake was an avid horticulturist who amassed 2,500 different plant species from all over the world for her ten-acre property. Its formal gardens were largely planned by her sister, Mabel Symmes, who

A water lily pool and a grotto/stairway front the Blake house's main entry.

studied landscape architecture at Berkeley. The house was deeded to the university in 1957, and since 1967 it has served as the official residence of the university's president. The grounds now serve as the Department of Landscape Architecture's outdoor laboratory and as a source of enjoyment and enlightenment for the public.

In addition to the breathtaking vistas, another special dividend of meandering among the hills and terraces of this estate is discovering its many rare, mature plant specimens. These number a copper beech, a hawthorne, Canary Island pines, acacias, New Zealand lacebark, redwoods (*Sequoia sempervirens*), and *Melaleuca styphelioides*, an Australian native with wonderful parchment-like bark. Among the memorable architectural features of the formal gardens is a long pool terminating with a grotto and lined with a double row of magnolias. Built in 1926, it is reminiscent of a similar design at the Villa Tusculana in Frascati, Italy.

Golden California poppies enliven a Regional Parks woodland setting.

REGIONAL PARKS BOTANIC GARDEN
Berkeley

Imagine California's 160,000 square miles reduced to a ten-acre garden that can be absorbed in a day. This botanic garden, situated in Berkeley's Tilden Regional Park, offers a microcosm of the vast territory's native flora, including examples of all its conifers, nearly all its oaks, and the most complete collections of its manzanitas and ceanothuses to be found anywhere. The garden's organization into sections representing the state's diverse natural environments—Southern California, Shasta-Cascade, Valley, Santa Lucia, Channel Islands, Sierran, Redwood, Sea Bluff, Pacific Rain Forest, and Franciscan—makes it possible to take a walk from the Oregon border in the north to the Mexican in the south, with botanical wonders unfolding all the way. More than 1,500 species, including wildflowers and outstanding specimens of giant sequoia and redwood, are arranged in delightful naturalistic settings that are interesting and informative all year. Beginning around mid-December and early January, they furnish a succession of bloom that continues uninterrupted for seven months.

Opening on January 1, 1940, the garden was founded and designed by James Roof, who had been working for the U.S. Forest Service germinating and propagating California native plants for erosion control and landscaping in the state's 18 national forests. The forest service, in fact, supplied the botanic garden, operated and maintained by East Bay Regional Park District, with its initial plant stock.

UNIVERSITY OF CALIFORNIA AT BERKELEY BOTANICAL GARDEN
Berkeley

Established in 1890 and moved to its present location in Strawberry Canyon in the 1920s, the remarkably diverse UC Berkeley Botanical Garden covers 33 acres with 10,000 species and varieties of plants from all over the world, making it the fifth largest such collection in the United States. Its beautifully landscaped setting is enhanced by the sight and sound of the cascades and pools of Strawberry Creek.

The garden's plant acquisitions, all "wild-collected" (grown from seeds or cuttings obtained from populations in the wild), are arranged according to region of origin, with more than one-third of the total made up of California natives. Wandering paths, affording wonderful views of San Francisco Bay and the city skyline, encounter a survey of the world's floral ecosystems: Southern African, with lilies, ice plants, and aloes; New World Desert, containing cacti and succulents from North and Central America, including the Andes; Asian/Japanese Pool, featuring an outstanding collection of rhododendrons; Australian/New Zealand, with eucalyptus, proteas, and podocarps; South American, inhabited by monkey puzzle trees, an exceptional collection of fuchsias and several Antarctic beech trees; Mediterranean/European, with its wild relatives of North American garden perennials and a rock garden of sempervivums; and Mesoamerican, featuring Mexican pines and oaks and a large Mexican handflower tree. As if that were not enough to satisfy the appetites of the most avid plantsmen,

Peruvian lilies supply a rainbow of color at the UC Berkeley garden.

there are collections of palms and cycads, a Garden of Old Roses, both Western and Chinese Medicinal Herb Gardens, and three greenhouses devoted to tropicals, desert and rain forest plants, and ferns and insectivorous species.

The facility was originally established as a source of study and research in the late 1800s at the instigation of Eugene W. Hilgard, the father of plant science at the Berkeley campus. Its strong educational tradition is reflected in the classes, tours, and other programs it offers today to the general public "to increase [its] appreciation of the diversity, value and beauty of the plant kingdom." As a member of the Center for Plant Conservation, a national consortium of botanical gardens and arboreta, the institution establishes cultivated collections of rare and endangered species from northern California and propagates these for research and reintroduction into the wild. Membership in the Garden's California Native Plant Society is open to all.

Leafing-out willows and other budding trees greet spring at Greystone Park.

GREYSTONE PARK
Beverly Hills

On a high ridge separating Los Angeles from the San Fernando Valley and affording spectacular vistas of Catalina island to the west and the snow-topped mountains to the east, the Greystone Mansion features wonderful gardens on its 19-acre grounds. Old trees, lawns, formal areas, and flower-filled beds are reminders of the grandeur of the film colony's heyday. The manor house is closed to the public, but the gardens offer a tranquil diversion from the beaten path, and on a clear day, incomparable views of the unique splendor of California's mountain- and seascapes.

VIRGINIA ROBINSON GARDENS
Beverly Hills

At a cul-de-sac some distance up the hills behind the Beverly Hills Hotel sits a house that is typical of those owned by film-industry stars of the 1920s and 1930s. In fact, it was Beverly Hills' very first residence, built in 1908, when the posh community could boast of no more than some barley fields and a real estate office. That was what Virginia Robinson liked to tell people, right up until she died in 1977 just weeks before her 100th birthday. The structure was designed, in the style of a Mediterranean villa, by Mrs. Robinson's father, architect Nathaniel Dryden, for his daughter and her new husband, Harry Robinson, heir to Robinson's department store.

The young couple traveled frequently to Europe, returning with an appreciation of the classical gardens of England, France, and Italy and seeds of rare, exotic plants. These flourished and the setting they lovingly created has been preserved today in all its lush, sultry, almost jungle-like splendor.

A bower of stephanotis and airy cosmos festoons a gateway at Robinson.

On a too-hurried visit while in Los Angeles on other business, I felt as if I had been transported to Hollywood in its heyday, half expecting Clark Gable and Carole Lombard to come bounding out of the pool house any second. This structure is situated in the formal, classic section of the grounds, at the end of an expansive lawn lined with annual borders and rows of towering Italian cypress. Surrounding this area at various levels are the more naturalized plantings, including camellias (a favorite of Mrs. Robinson's, in bloom in late January), azaleas, Southern magnolias, citrus trees, roses, the largest monkey hand tree in California, and the biggest stand of king palms outside Australia.

Harry Robinson died in 1932. Upon her death, Mrs. Robinson, having no heirs, left her property under the care of the County of Los Angeles.

The vivid red of Christmas berry, or toyon (Heteromeles), *cheers a wintry trail in the naturalized area of Rancho Santa Ana Botanic Garden.*

RANCHO SANTA ANA BOTANIC GARDEN
Claremont

Devoted entirely to plants native to the state of California, this well-organized research and educational institution displays about 1,500 different species. At its present site since 1951, the garden was originally located at historic Rancho Santa Ana in Orange County, where it was founded in 1927 by Susanna Bixby Bryant in memory of her father, John W. Bixby. The aims of the facility are to preserve the native flora of the state, to promote their horticultural use, and to select and test the suitability of their cultivars for landscaping purposes. Offering a broad range of educational programs both for schoolchildren and adults, the garden is a private institution wholly dependent on gifts and an endowment.

With the spectacular San Gabriel Mountains crowning the beauty of its 80 some odd acres, the living collection is organized into two 40-acre sections: a trail-accessed naturalized area where examples are grouped according to the plant communities in which they are found in the wild, and a series of thoughtfully planned theme gardens that are spread out handsomely over the top of a mesa.

Among the latter are: the Desert Garden, with succulents, shrubs, and all of the state's cactus species; the Coastal Garden, where dune and island habitats are re-created; the Riparian Trail, with deciduous trees and water-loving plants set alongside a stream and pond; the Conifer Collection, containing half of the 54 species that grow in the state whose conifers number among them the earth's oldest living trees; the Home Demonstration Garden, displaying landscaping ideas, especially the use of drought-tolerant native species and cultivars; the Manzanita Display Areas, where these popular native plants, with mid-December-through-February flowers and all-year, red-tinged foliage, show off their suitability as a groundcover; the Ceanothus (California Lilac) Collection, offering the abundance and variety of bloom (from early March to late April) that make it one of the major attractions of the garden; and Wildflowers, carpeting the mesa from mid-March through the end of May with California poppies, meadow-foam, gilias, brodiaeas, and clarkias, among others.

SHERMAN LIBRARY AND GARDENS
Corona del Mar

Sherman Library and Gardens is a unique repository of lore surrounding the development of the Pacific Southwest in the last 100 years. Echoing early California architecture, its buildings, including an adobe house built in 1940, offer a library research facility and lively exhibits explaining how and why the area developed as rapidly as it did. An unusual use of complete lath structures over greenhouses provides necessary shade and, along with connecting pergola-covered walkways, unifies the design of the complex.

Named in memory of Moses H. Sherman (1853–1932), a California pioneer and educator, the center is home to a botanic garden that is virtually a living museum of tropical, subtropical, and desert plants from around the world. More than 1,000 species and over 200 genera are represented. Three color gardens dotted with pools and fountains ensure beds of flowers all year. Red, pink, and white dianthus radiate in summer, while winter and early spring find the beds filled with tulips, primroses, and Iceland poppies. Encountered among the remainder of the gardens are: a fern grotto with giant staghorn and moosehorn examples; a desert garden with cacti and succulents; a shade garden with an assortment of begonias; a rose garden; a conservatory housing orchids, carnivorous

A Sherman Gardens summer display of nicotiana (near) and dianthus (far).

plants, bromeliads, and anthuriums, and a tea garden hung with baskets spilling over with delicately pendulous fuchsias and angel's trumpets. The Discovery Garden concentrates on plantings designed specifically for the blind and for wheelchair navigation.

The library and gardens were begun in 1966 by the Sherman Foundation under the leadership of its principal benefactor, Arnold D. Haskell (1896–1977). Continued operation of the facility depends on private grants and membership support.

UNIVERSITY OF CALIFORNIA AT DAVIS ARBORETUM
Davis

Situated 15 miles west of Sacramento, this 100-acre preserve within the UC Davis campus concentrates on plants amenable to the climate of California's great Central Valley, including the largest stand of coast redwoods outside their natural habitats. The unrestrained natural beauty of the parklike setting, with its beneficent old trees, is made all the more exuberant by Putah Creek, bisecting the site and flourishing with waterfowl, fish, and turtles. The collections gravitate toward plants indigenous to California and include some of the state's most engaging spring wildflowers.

The Carolee Shields Garden, a circular design surrounding a gazebo, is a haunting all-white garden, planted with white-flowering vines and shrubs and silver-leaved foliage plants exclusively. Such gardens are particularly engaging on a clear, moonlit night, and throughout history have been designed to capture the nocturnal light. The setting is named for the late arboretum benefactor who grew only white flowers in her own garden. The 15-acre Peter J. Shields Oak Grove, dedicated to the California Superior Court judge who was a lifelong horticulturist, contains more than 70 species, both native and imported, of the over 450 that comprise this mighty tree genus. The Ruth Risdon Storer Garden, honoring a devoted horticulturist and 60-year resident of Davis who grows its most consistently beautiful garden, is designed to glow with color all year. Plantings of grape hyacinths, pinks, snow-in-summer, herbaceous perennials, all kinds of lavenders, grey-leaved plants, rock roses (*Cistus*), and California fuchsias (*Zauschneria cana*) offer an outstanding, yet delicate, array of bloom. This garden also offers displays of water-conserving, drought-tolerant plants.

The arboretum's Outdoor Education Program helps children learn to appreciate the beauty and value of nature. Volunteers assist in all activities, including growing plants for the annual rare-plant sale. Supporters of the institution through membership in the Friends of the Davis Arboretum receive discounts on tours and workshops, a newsletter, and many other opportunities and privileges.

Sedum rhodanthum, *a water-thrifty native akin to those at Davis Arboretum.*

QUAIL BOTANICAL GARDENS
Encinitas

The sunny hillsides and deep canyons of Quail Botanical Gardens, within view of the Pacific Ocean, invite visitors to experience the plant environments of the desert, the Himalayas, the South Pacific, South Africa, Central America, and Australia. Winding trails encounter rich samplings, in succession, of the world's most unusual and exotic cacti and succulents, palms, ferns, and intoxicatingly fragrant flowers. Blessed with the subtropical, nearly frost-free climate of southern California, this 25-acre preserve is host to the largest hibiscus collection (28 species, 84 cultivars) on the West Coast and more bamboos (52 species) than anywhere else in the United States.

In the 1930s Charles and Ruth Baird Larabee bought a parcel of land on an eroded ridge, its sandy soil supporting scant native vegetation. As an avid plant collector, Mrs. Larabee gathered select species from all over the globe, with an emphasis on those from Central and South America, and it was not very long before the property, aptly dubbed *El Rancho de las Flores*, was transformed. In 1957 Mrs. Larabee deeded her creation to the County of San Diego which has since developed the collection, through the efforts of the Quail Botanical Gardens Foundation, into one of the most diverse and botanically significant in the country. It was designated a unit of the San Diego County Parks and Recreation Department in 1959.

Cascading water splashes a diversity of tropicals at Quail Botanical.

The gardens are well-known for their extensive collections of cycads, aloes, daylilies, fuchsias, philodendrons, and proteas. Theme installations include the Walled, Subtropical Fruit, Herb, and Old Fashioned Gardens and the Mildred MacPherson Waterfall, a 150-foot-long man-made cascade dropping a total of 50 feet and hugged with such tropicals as gingers, abutilons, alstroemerias, bromeliads, and brugmansias (angel's trumpet). A variety of horticulture-related activities and events are hosted at the Ecke Building, donated, along with four additional acres of land, by Paul and Magdalena Ecke in 1971.

Heather (Calluna vulgaris) *supplies winter color at Mendocino Botanical.*

MENDOCINO COAST BOTANICAL GARDENS
Fort Bragg

Containing thousands of kinds of native and introduced plants, this botanical garden benefits immeasurably from the spectacular beauty of California's rocky Mendocino coastline. Laced by more than two miles of trails, some enjoying magnificent views of the ocean, the principal collections to be found on six acres of this 17-acre facility include drought-tolerant plants, dwarf conifers, tender-species rhododendrons (in bloom in April and May), perennials (May to October), camellias and heathers (winter), and succulents. The major gardens include a rhododendron dell, a rose garden, and a bog garden. Serving as habitats for enormous varieties of wildlife and waterfowl, including the great blue heron, the gardens' remaining 11 acres include coastal forests of native pine and Digger Creek's fern-bedecked canyon. A retail nursery on the premises offers a wide variety of plants for sale.

KRUSE RHODODENDRON STATE RESERVE
Fort Ross

Located within Salt Point State Park and scattered throughout 320 acres of a forest of Douglas firs and redwoods, this preserve of native rhododendrons is in magnificent bloom from March through May, with April marking the peak. The state park facilities include picnic areas, campgrounds, and hiking trails for extended enjoyment of this enormous and inspiring natural preserve along the breathtaking Northern California coast.

The spring bloom of native rhododendrons draws visitors to Kruse Reserve.

FULLERTON ARBORETUM
Fullerton

Covering 26 acres at the northeast corner of California State University's Fullerton campus, this informative, family-oriented arboretum represents the cooperative efforts of the university, the community, and various private groups and individuals. Opened to the public in 1979, the facility serves not only as a resource for education, research, and conservation, but as an inviting, restful retreat in the midst of a dynamic urban area. Somewhat of a departure from other institutions of its kind is the fact that its plant collections from around the world are grouped ecologically according to moisture requirements, with an emphasis on drought-tolerant choices. A waterfall, stream, and ponds along the western end of the site create an ideal environment for temperate- and tropical-zone plants, as well as a sanctuary for waterfowl, fish, and turtles, while dryland plants flourish in the north and east sections of the grounds. These are further divided into the Palm Garden, the Subtropical Fruit Grove, the Conifer Area, the Cactus & Succulent Garden, the Carnivorous Plant Bog, and an area reserved for flower and vegetable community gardens. The Rose Garden, with a gazebo, is devoted primarily to hybrid teas, but many favorite old varieties, such as China roses, are included. The Historical Orchard focuses on avocados, oranges, and walnuts of economic importance to the early development of Orange County.

Also to be found at Fullerton is a charmingly designed wisteria arbor, where weddings are often held, and a Victorian Cottage furnished in the style of the period and known as Heritage House. Built in 1894 as the home and office of Fullerton's first physician and moved to the arboretum in 1972, the restored abode, listed in the National Register of Historic Places, is a museum of early medical practice. Its gardens feature planting designs appropriate to the period, including annuals and scented geraniums in its Entry Garden and vegetables and herbs in raised beds in its

A hedgehog cactus blooms among other delights of Fullerton's Cactus Garden.

1890s-style Kitchen Garden. Of special fascination for children is a thriving apiary. Its hard-working bees demonstrate their role in pollination, and their honey is sold in the arboretum gift shop.

Offering workshops, demonstrations, and seminars throughout the year, Fullerton also maintains a public research library. The Friends of the Fullerton Arboretum Society, with open membership, lends the institution financial and volunteer support.

The fiery bloom of Aloe africana *salutes UC Irvine's vast collection.*

UNIVERSITY OF CALIFORNIA AT IRVINE ARBORETUM
Irvine

Situated in one of the world's five ecosystems designated as Mediterranean, the UCI Arboretum naturally gravitated toward an interest in plants originating from these tropical and subtropical regions. A lath house, bulb house, greenhouse, and South African shrub and sand dune gardens present a fascinating collection of cacti and succulents, particularly aloes and South African bulbous and cormous plants. The latter, representing one of the finest assemblages in the country, include many rare and endangered species of such genera as *Gladiolus, Babiana, Ixia, Moraea, Cyrtanthus*, and *Lachenalia*.

The installation originated in 1964 as a nursery established to supply the new Irvine campus with plants for its landscaping. It functioned for a time as an experimental garden before its official development as an arboretum began in 1976. With a worldwide reputation in plant conservation, the institution grows and propagates nearly 200 endangered species and maintains a gene bank, in which pollen and seed from thousands more are stored at subzero temperatures. Membership in the university's Friends Society supports its efforts at saving the world's exotic flora.

DESCANSO GARDENS
La Cañada Flintridge

Descanso Gardens is a camellia showplace in spring. It contains the largest known forest, more than 100,000 trees representing 600 varieties, of these exquisitely showy bloomers.

One of four public gardens comprising the County of Los Angeles Department of Arboreta and Botanic Gardens, Descanso covers 165 acres, 55 of which consist of cultivated gardens open to the public. I was especially taken with the way the planned gardens are nestled against towering

The Chinese red of an authentic Oriental bridge glows in the deep shade of a Descanso Gardens forest and outlines a stand of agapanthus.

hills, lending all of Descanso a picturesque scenic backdrop. Color throughout the year is provided by a wide variety of annuals and perennials. More than six miles of hiking trails lend access to a History of Roses Garden (containing among its species some that have been in cultivation since 1200 B.C.) and a Japanese teahouse, offering pools, waterfalls, beds of azaleas, and ceremonial servings of tea.

The property was originally the home of the owner of the Los Angeles *Daily News*, E. Manchester Boddy (who named the site Rancho Del Descanso, or Ranch of Rest), until 1953 when it was purchased by the County of Los Angeles. The white-pillared, antebellum-style mansion that Boddy built for himself is now a gallery of fine art, offering shows that change monthly.

The Descanso Gardens Guild, Inc., a nonprofit organization, oversees the preservation and promotion of the gardens.

Sempervivums are among the Miller Garden's abundant dry-climate succulents.

THE HORTENSE MILLER GARDEN
Laguna Beach

In a picturesque seaside community that has always reminded me of the hillside hamlets along the French and Italian rivieras, Hortense Miller has created a 2½-acre paradise. This public-spirited horticulturist has generously opened her home garden on the upper slopes of Boat Canyon to visitors, by appointment, through the auspices of the Laguna Beach city management. The exuberant plantings developed over the years now encompass more than 1,200 species, ranging from the exotics of the subtropical regions of the world through longtime favorites of the temperate zones of the native vegetation of coastal Southern California. Offering living testament to the enormous range of plants that can be grown in this area of the country, the garden is a rich source of ideas and inspiration for its many loyal admirers.

Devoted to the preservation of California coastal sage scrub, the northwestern half of the site remains unbowed by a devastating brush fire in 1979. The lemonade berry, or rhus, has returned to its former dominance, regrowing from root crowns, as has the California holly, or toyon. Paths through this area wander among scatterings of black sage, California sagebrush, bush monkey flower, and wild buckwheat. Small glades and clearings are each planted with one or a few genera of bush lupines, penstemon, Douglas irises, blue-eyed grass, and other native perennials. Shady and moist areas play host to mushrooms, lichens, and native ferns.

Dry-climate plants, including a rare tree euphorbia, several eucalyptuses, and a wide assortment of other succulents grow in one of the many pocket gardens defined by the spreading wings of the house. A steep slope covered with lampranthus presents a profusion of bloom in late spring, and an inner patio offers the surprise of a quaint gazebo traced with the vines of an old 'Mermaid' rose. Found throughout the property are bountiful cascades of more flowering vines, including jasmine, Japanese wisteria, and Easter-lily vine (*Beaumontia grandiflora*). Mature trees and flowering shrubs, a perennial garden, and bulb plantings, including stands of amaryllis and crinum lilies, are more of the delights to be discovered in this mini-Eden on the Pacific.

The Friends of The Hortense Miller Garden, with membership open to all, is a nonprofit corporation devoted to the continuing support and improvement of the garden.

RANCHO LOS ALAMITOS HISTORIC SITE AND GARDENS
Long Beach

A surviving testament to the dynamic growth of ranching and farming in Southern California, Rancho Los Alamitos is dominated by a sprawling ranch house filled with period furnishings. Dating from 1790 and expanded through 1933, the adobe structure is the oldest dwelling of its kind to be found in the state. Its four acres of landscaped grounds reflect the relaxed and unpretentious quality of California ranch life in its late nineteenth-century heyday. First developed during that era by Susan Bixby, the gardens as they exist today owe more to the efforts of her daughter-in-law, Florence Green Bixby, who infused them with her own distinct personality and sensitivity between the years 1910 and 1930. The Rose

Garden, Oleander Walk, Herb Garden, Desert and Native Gardens, and the Friendly Garden, representing the talent of such designers as Florence Yoch, William Hertrich and Charles Gibb Adams, lend the impression of a succession of outdoor rooms. Plantings of pepper trees, wisteria, jacaranda, Cape honeysuckle, plumbago, Canary Island date palm, Moreton Bay fig, aloes, and jades, all typically found in early twentieth-century California gardens, are distinguished here by their elegant maturity and attractive placement.

In addition to the main house, the grounds encompass six early twentieth-century barns and a working blacksmith shop. Deeded to the City of Long Beach in 1968 as a gift from the Fred H. Bixby family, the ranch was first opened to the public in 1970. Rancho Los Alamitos Foundation, a nonprofit organization, has managed and operated the site as a public/private cooperative effort with the City of Long Beach since 1986.

An aged ficus lends dramatic form to Rancho Los Alamitos' landscape.

MILDRED E. MATHIAS BOTANICAL GARDEN
Los Angeles

A broad spectrum of tropical and subtropical plants for the edification of students and visitors alike are on view in the eight acres that comprise this University of California display garden. A visit one bright summer day filled me with wonder at the myriad and fascinating diversity of forms that make up our planet's flora. The collection of cacti and succulents alone at

Fascinating denizens of the desert are in rare form at UC's Mathias Garden.

this facility underscores the resourceful adaptability and creativity of nature's handiwork, and the degree to which most ornamental gardening clings to just a tiny fraction of the many plants it could be making use of.

The garden was established as an academic laboratory in 1930, shortly after the university moved to its Westwood location. It was renamed in 1979 in honor of Dr. Mildred E. Mathias, a botanist at UCLA since 1947 and director of the garden from 1956 to 1974. A total of 4,000 species representing 225 plant families are grown on the facility both for display and to determine how well these choices adapt to the Southern California climate.

In addition to being sectioned into major classifications of plants to make students and visitors aware of relatedness, the garden is organized according to specific themes. These include: Lily Beds, with true lilies from every continent; Cycad Section; Tropical American Highlands, with species from Central and South America; Rhododendron Beds; Australian Section, with a wide range of eucalyptus; Gymnosperms; Palm Section; Aquatic Section; California Section; and Desert Garden.

UCLA HANNAH CARTER JAPANESE GARDEN
Los Angeles

Reminiscent of the gardens of Kyoto, this tranquil, 1½-acre Japanese-style landscape tucked among the hills of Bel Air was created in 1961 by Mr. and Mrs. Gordon Guiberson in memory of Mr. Guiberson's mother, Ethel

Exotic water lilies enrich the UCLA Carter Garden's Oriental mood.

L. Guiberson, organizer of the Beverly Hills Garden Club. Having studied many Japanese gardens, the sublime examples in Kyoto among them, the Guibersons engaged Nagao Sakurai to design one in this residential community within Los Angeles.

The major structures found in the garden—the main gate, teahouse, bridges, and shrine—were built in Japan and reassembled here by Japanese artisans. Symbolic boulders, antique stone carvings, and water basins were also shipped to the site from Japan. Dispersed among these are 400 tons of lichen-covered, dark brown stone gathered at Santa Paula Canyon in Ventura County. Native California live oaks, antedating the garden, have been left to play host only to trees and shrubs typically grown in Japan.

Serving as a teaching laboratory for several UCLA departments, the garden was donated to the institution in 1965 by Edward W. Carter, then chairman of the University Regents.

THE J. PAUL GETTY MUSEUM
Malibu

A step backward in time to the glory of ancient Rome is in store for the visitor to the J. Paul Getty Museum. Confronted with the sheer perfection of detail and opulence of materials of this magnificent creation one typically sunny California day in summer, I was in awe of the accomplishments of the Romans and of the renowned collector who recaptured them for the modern-day public.

The late J. Paul Getty, having lived most of his life in Europe, amassed an enormous collection of Greek and Roman antiquities, Renaissance and

Baroque paintings, and European decorative arts. He established a museum for his collection in 1953 at his house in Malibu. But by the mid-1960s, the collection was rapidly outgrowing these accommodations, so Mr. Getty commissioned a brand-new building that was to be a re-creation of the Villa dei Papiri. This sprawling Roman house and gardens, overlooking the Bay of Naples at ancient Herculaneum, was completely buried by the eruption of nearby Mt. Vesuvius in A.D. 79. Notes and floor plans derived from eighteenth-century tunneling (the villa remains underground to this day) formed the basis for the museum's design. All of the plantings installed were also representative of what would have been grown at the original villa. The Getty was opened to the public in January of 1974.

An extensive colonnade surrounding a garden with a huge reflecting pool, fountains, and statuary is the stunning first sight that confronts the visitor. Roses, oleander, and beds delineated with the most perfectly manicured boxwood hedges I have ever seen form the basic natural elements of this massive entryway. The scent of grapes is deliciously overwhelming as one passes beneath the pergolas supporting the fruit's clambering vines. At the core of the house itself is an atrium garden, and outside to the east is a smaller walled garden. To the west, a series of terraces accommodates the museum's outdoor café, with tables and chairs shaded by pergolas artfully strung with garlands of living ivy. To the south of the café is a long, narrow herb garden of ancient design.

Oleanders and ancient statuary share the lime-light at The Getty.

Ferns thrive in the moist shade of Muir Woods' giant redwoods.

MUIR WOODS NATIONAL MONUMENT
Mill Valley

Muir Woods, part of the Golden Gate National Recreation Area, is a 560-acre forest of coast redwoods, one of the last remaining preserves of these magnificent examples of nature's handiwork. Until the 1800s when they fell victim to the logging industry, these trees, some as old as 1,000 years and standing 300 feet tall, covered most of Northern California's coastal valleys. Recognizing that this particular stand of old-growth redwood, along Redwood Creek, 17 miles from San Francisco, represented the Bay Area's last, Congressman William Kent and his wife, Elizabeth Thatcher Kent, bought a 295-acre tract in 1905 and donated it to the Federal Government. In 1908 President Theodore Roosevelt declared the area a national monument, suggesting that it be named in honor of William Kent. But Kent insisted that it be given the name of a courageous protector of the wilderness at that time, conservationist, scientist, and author John Muir.

The towering presences of the redwoods, some with trunks as wide as 14 feet, and the cathedral-like serenity of the eternally shaded forest canyon provide an awe-inspiring experience. Lingering in the giants' shadows, other trees to be discovered along the miles of trails include Douglas-fir, big-leaf maple, tanbark oak, bay-laurel, red alder, and buckeye. Thriving in the moisture-laden valley are an abundance of ferns, including sword fern, ladyfern, California polypody, and bracken fern. A fascinating assortment of mosses, lichens, and mushrooms cling to live and dead tree trunks.

Informative exhibits within the preserve include: a cross-cut section of trunk revealing its growth layers and its age as it relates to historical events; a self-guiding, marked nature trail; an explanation of how the trees naturally propagate and how periodic flooding of the creek provides the vast amounts of water they require; and a comparison of the various kinds of redwoods: the coast redwood (*Sequoia sempervirens*), the giant sequoia (*Sequoiadendron giganteum*), restricted to the Sierra Nevadas' western slopes, and the dawn redwood (*Metasequoia glyptostroboides*), native to a remote area of China.

Muir Woods National Monument is operated under the auspices of the National Park Service of the United States Department of the Interior.

A bank of California daisies (Euryops) *greets visitors to Dunsmuir.*

DUNSMUIR HOUSE AND GARDENS
Oakland

The 1889 white, porticoed example of Victorian Colonial-Revival architecture that impressively presides over this restored estate represents a fascinating tale of unrequited love. Alexander Dunsmuir, the son of a successful coal and lumber baron (James Dunsmuir—see Hatley Park, p. 127) and the brother of the Prime Minister of British Columbia, commissioned the building of the mansion as a wedding gift for his young bride, Josephine.

But while on his honeymoon, Alexander died, leaving his wife to return to her new home alone. The bereaved widow never recovered from her loss, was overcome by illness, and died herself in 1901. It was I. W. Hellman, Jr., of the Wells Fargo Bank and purchaser of the estate in 1906, and his wife Frances, who realized Alexander Dunsmuir's dream for the development of the property. It flourished and prospered under the name of Oakvale Park until Frances Hellman's death in 1959, when it was sold to the City of Oakland, with the hope that it would be preserved as a reminder of the opulence of a bygone era. The 37-room mansion features wood-paneled rooms, inlaid parquet floors, and a Tiffany-glass dome over the entrance hallway. Outlying structures on the estate include a gazebo, a carriage house, a dairy barn, a potting shed, a grotto, and a children's log-cabin playhouse.

Only partially representative of the splendor of what once existed in the way of gardens, the grounds' 48 acres are distinguished by mature hornbeam, copper beech, cottonwood, black locust, and live oak trees, a cactus and succulent garden, an arbor draped with wisteria, and hundreds of kinds of flowering trees, shrubs, and perennials. Though now in ruin, the Japanese garden that once graced the site is still in evidence and remains to be restored. Christmas is celebrated at Dunsmuir with period decorations and thousands of lights adorning the mansion facade.

LAKESIDE PARK GARDEN CENTER
Oakland

One of America's most user-friendly municipal parks, 120-acre Lakeside Park borders Lake Merritt, Oakland's inland saltwater lake. All kinds of recreational facilities, including an amusement park for children that is said to have been the prototype for Disneyland, a natural science center, and a bandstand offering concerts, are available within the confines of this attractive facility. More to the point for those interested in gardens and plants is the park's six-acre Garden Center, with annual and perennial trial gardens, a conservatory filled with tropicals, a Japanese Garden, a fragrance garden for the blind, home demonstration gardens, and inspiring collections of camellias, dahlias, fuchsias, roses, and tuberous begonias.

Throughout the year the center sponsors a variety of garden shows. Mounted in association with the local chapters of the related national plant societies, these exhibits feature, among others: bonsai (October and April), fuchsias (November), lilies (December), rhododendrons (March-April), irises (April), roses (May), orchids (May), dahlias (September), cacti and succulents (September), and African violets (September–October). At each show, bulbs, tubers, or full-grown specimens of the featured plant are offered for sale, new varieties are presented, and in some cases, home-grown specimens are entered for judging.

Plantings at Lakeside's Visitor Center hint at the park's diversity.

THE OAKLAND MUSEUM AND GARDENS
Oakland

One of the country's most innovative architectural designs and museum concepts, the Oakland Museum is a maze of multileveled galleries topped with terraces and gardens. Reminiscent of the Hanging Gardens of Babylon, the unique complex is the creation of architect Kevin Roche who sought to relieve the usual tedium of one identical gallery after another with hidden patios, surprise spaces, and lush plantings. Lively, colorful, and contributing to the festival atmosphere, the museum's exhibits are devoted to a California theme, presenting the Golden State's history, science, artistic expression, and cultural diversity. Rising in tiers from a spacious central plaza of lawn, trees, and a pond, four main levels embrace 17 smaller courts planted with a diverse sampling of unusual groundcovers, cascading vines, and flowering trees and shrubs. An automatic irrigation system supplies water and fertilizer and two special soil mixes developed at the University of California insure lightness and optimum drainage. Visitors may stroll from one terrace to another, relax and enjoy the gardens from built-in benches, or take in the picturesque view of nearby Lake Merritt.

Opened in 1969, the museum brings together the traditions and disciplines of three former Oakland institutions: the Oakland Public Museum (founded in 1910), devoted primarily to Native American and American history, the Oakland Art Museum (founded in 1916), and the Snow Museum of Natural History (founded in 1922). Financial support is provided by the City of Oakland and the Oakland Museum Association, a nonprofit membership organization.

Koi cavort amid sculpture and aquatic plants at The Oakland Museum.

THE LIVING DESERT
Palm Desert

Just as an aquarium provides access to the living creatures of the sea, this unique attraction presents the flora and fauna of the desert in all their wondrous variety and endless mechanisms for adapting to the forbidding extremes of heat, cold, and scarcity of water. More than 7,000 individual plants representing 1,500 desert species constitute the most comprehensive collection of its kind in Southern California. These are arranged in naturalistic re-creations of nine North American dryland regions, inviting close inspection of prehistoric cycads, subtropic desert willows, exotic alluadia from Madagascar, giant saguaros, smoketrees, Joshua trees (yuccas), and hundreds of blooming cacti.

Striking cactus (Rebutia) *blooms allude to The Living Desert's exotic beauty.*

Among the many educational exhibits is one that explains the subtle, yet distinct, differences between cacti, native only to the New World, and cactus-like euphorbias. Another enumerates ways to use these and other fascinating desert plants in the home landscape. The Cahuilla Indian garden contains the traditional dwelling (a kish) of these resourceful local natives and the plants they relied on for food, fiber, medicine, and building material. At the nursery within the grounds, thousands of native desert species are propagated for planting in the gardens and for sale to visitors.

The facility's 1,200 acres accommodate a nature preserve that enables all kinds of wildlife to roam free in settings akin to their natural habitats. On view are slenderhorn gazelle, Arabian oryx, coyotes, meerkats, tortoises, gila monsters, foxes, and other denizens of the desert, 60 species in all. Winged varieties fly at liberty in a large walk-through aviary.

Founded in 1970 by Philip Boyd as a 360-acre wilderness preserve with interpretive nature trails, The Living Desert has expanded considerably over the years in its ongoing dedication to conservation, education, and research related to the desert environment. As a nonprofit institution, it relies solely on memberships, contributions, and admissions.

MOORTEN BOTANICAL GARDEN
Palm Springs

Moorten Botanical Garden, also known as "Desertland," is a living gallery of the myriad and curious forms of cacti and other desert plants. I never cease to be amazed at the outlandish growth habits, endless variety, and fiesta-color flowers of these fascinating plants, and once wrote a book on the subject. But to encounter unique cacti and other succulents in the flesh for yourself, this two-acre installation in the desert of Palm Springs is the place to go. Arranged according to various dryland regions of the world, the garden is divided into Sonoran, Mojave, Yuman, Californian, Mexican, African, and South American deserts. Inhabiting these various areas are more than 3,000 kinds of drought-tolerant plants, including giant saguaro, organ pipe, prickly pear, and barrel cacti, yuccas, agaves, an ocotillo forest, and the ironwood tree, yielding the hardest wood known. Children will especially enjoy the Old West artifacts and pioneer relics sprinkled along the trails and lending plenty of atmosphere. Adding to their fascination is the fact that some are props left over from westerns filmed in the area.

Patricia Moorten, who established the collection in 1938 and moved it to its present location in 1955 with her late husband, Chester "Cactus Slim" Moorten, remains its director today. She is vastly knowledgeable about cactus lore, having written her own book on the subject and having cultivated thousands of cacti for shipment to botanical gardens throughout the world. Plants grown at the facility are offered to visitors for purchase at the nursery. The Moorten residence on the grounds, originally built for artist Stephen Willard in 1929, is an appropriate Spanish-style house that is itself a curiosity. Intended to be earthquake-proof, it is unshakably fashioned of poured concrete and steel beams, with walls 2-feet thick.

Dryland trees and opuntia cacti await investigation at Moorten.

Gamble Garden Center's raised planter boxes invite tending by gardeners in wheelchairs. Note the old-fashioned latticework fence.

ELIZABETH F. GAMBLE GARDEN CENTER
Palo Alto

The charm of the New England colonies makes its way to the West Coast in the Colonial-Revival home and carriage house built in 1902 for Edwin Percy Gamble. The homestead's formal gardens, designed by Walter A. Hoff, include such traditional touches as a rose garden, a wisteria pergola, a grotto, and shrub and perennial borders. In 1948 Mr. Gamble's daughter, Elizabeth, added a teahouse, and improved the gardens according to a plan by Allan Reid. In 1981 Miss Gamble gave the estate to the City of Palo Alto whose City Council in 1985 approved leasing it to the Elizabeth F. Gamble Garden Center Foundation.

With the help of the Palo Alto Garden Club and membership enrollment, a nonprofit corporation funds and administers the property as a horticultural center. Its rich and varied program of classes, lectures, workshops, and special events is enhanced by the window into the past that the gardens provide. Specimen oak trees, a weeping cherry allee, an iris border, a formal herb garden, a greenhouse, a slat house, and latticework fencing, among other features, all suggest the gentility and grace of another era, another place.

Bedded petunias carpet the ground with pink at South Coast Garden.

SOUTH COAST BOTANIC GARDEN
Palos Verdes Peninsula

Millions of years ago, the land that is now the Palos Verdes Peninsula was covered by the Pacific Ocean. As the water receded, the earth that emerged was highly diatomaceous, rich with algae fossil remains (called diatoms). Beginning in 1929, the site was mined for diatomite, until it was acquired by the County of Los Angeles in 1956 for the deposit of sanitary landfill. In 1959 the Los Angeles County Department of Arboreta and Botanic Gardens assumed the responsibility for planning, operating, and maintaining an 87-acre botanical garden on three-feet-deep topsoil above three-and-a-half million tons of refuse.

A startling example of creative land reclamation, the installation opened to the public in 1963. Today it boasts a lake, a meandering stream, display gardens, a wildlife habitat, and over 150,000 plants representing 700 genera and 2,000 species. Specialized gardens include: a shade garden, with fuchsias, impatiens, begonias, camellias, clivias, ferns, and gingers; herb and vegetable gardens; an English perennial garden; a desert garden, with cacti and succulents; and an orchard, with a variety of fruit trees and magnolias. Major plant collections include: dahlias (in bloom from June to September); roses (60 varieties); bromeliads; coral trees; redwoods; eucalyptus (50 species); conifers; palms; and ficus (20 species).

South Coast Botanic Garden Foundation, a nonprofit support group, provides additional funds and volunteers for the improvement and maintenance of the garden.

THE EDDY ARBORETUM
Placerville

Within the Institute of Forest Genetics, a research facility of the U.S. Forest Service, the Eddy Arboretum features a self-guided trail containing about 70 of the world's 95 species of pine, including the oldest verified hybrids made by man. Established in 1925 by James G. Eddy, an enterprising lumberman from the Pacific Northwest, the institute is the oldest facility in the world devoted to tree research and breeding. Inspired by Luther Burbank and adapting his hybridizing techniques, Eddy recognized the urgency of increasing forest production to meet the country's growing need for lumber and paper. In 1935 he donated the station to the U.S. Forest Service which has since used it to develop faster growing, straighter trees with good wood properties and resistance to insects and diseases. Declared a National Historic Site in 1987, the institute occupies 115 acres at an elevation of 2,700 feet in the foothills of the Sierra Nevada Mountains.

The Eddy offers high-altitude appreciation of 70 species of pines.

UNIVERSITY OF CALIFORNIA AT RIVERSIDE BOTANIC GARDENS
Riverside

Nestled in the Box Springs Mountains and occupying 39 acres along the eastern border of the UC Riverside campus, these picturesque gardens are a living museum of more than 3,000 plants from around the world. Memorable for its steep arroyos, huge granite boulders, and spectacular vistas of

Ground-covering ice plant is among the wonders at UC Riverside gardens.

the San Gabriel and San Bernardino mountains, the rugged, hilly terrain varies in elevation from 1,000 feet to 1,450 feet, encompassing a range of microclimates hospitable to a rare diversity of plants. Four miles of scenic trails wander among such highlights as: the Cactus and Succulent Gardens, alive with bloom and the curious forms of agaves, aloes, and euphorbias; cool and shady Alder Canyon, filled with azaleas, camellias, ferns, and winter daphne; the Iris Garden, featuring 150 named cultivars; the Rose Garden, with over 300 old and new selections, including miniatures; the Herb Garden, with its wide variety of aromatic, culinary, and medicinal choices; the Geodesic Lath Dome, sheltering a distinguished collection of cycads and palms; and the Subtropical Fruit Orchard, a demonstration and trial ground displaying a variety of fruiting trees.

The facility's first plants were installed in 1963 and with new additions every year since, the gardens now boast more than 2,500 species. The concentration is on plants indigenous to California, Australia, and southern Africa, with those native to California representing all quarters, from the deserts to the mountains, from the coastal hills to the inland valleys. The better known among the Australian genera include *Acacia*, *Callistemon*, *Eucalyptus* and *Grevillea*, and southern African natives account for most of the gardens' succulents. Aside from the global representatives, other collections include ficus trees and their citrus relatives and conifers, comprising pine, cypress, juniper, callitris, and araucaria species. Anytime of the year will find something abloom at Riverside, but the most colorful displays are rendered by camellias (October–May), aloes and ice plants (December–March), iris and lilacs (April and May), and roses (April–December).

MARIN ART AND GARDEN CENTER
Ross

In this unusual arboretum, old and rare specimen trees stand as living memorials to individuals who performed outstanding deeds, and in some cases have given their lives, in the service of their country. On a site that was once part of a Mexican land grant called Rancho Punto de Quentin and originally owned by James Ross, for whom the town is named, the center was founded in 1943 through the efforts of Mrs. Norman B. Livermore. Determined to preserve the site's magnificent trees, including a 65-foot-spread magnolia grandiflora, Mrs. Livermore brought together eight independent community groups to share in the purchase of the property and to establish an Art and Garden Center.

Among the magnificent trees to be found on the grounds' eight acres are: a giant sequoia dedicated to Marin County residents who lost their lives in World War II; a rare dawn redwood (see Muir Woods National Monument, p. 46) grown from a seed cone brought from China by paleontologist Dr. R. W. Chaney and donated by Ward Montague in memory of his wife, Alice; an enormous black oak endowed by Thomas Berry in memory of his brother, Tiernon Brien Berry; a golden locust dedicated to Roger F. Shoner, one of the first directors of the center; and a Japanese maple in memory of Isabella Worn. Other remarkable trees awaiting future dedication include a large English holly, a tulip tree, horse chestnuts, a ginkgo, a copper beech, and eastern-American elms and maples.

The property's art galleries and facilities for theatrical and concert performances are surrounded by lovely gardens featuring orchids, rhododendrons, and wisteria. The center is a community cooperative organization, operated on a nonprofit basis for the residents of Marin County.

Marin Art and Garden Center's Octagon House guards a restful pool.

BALBOA PARK
San Diego

On land that was originally dry mesas and canyons with brick-hard earth, Balboa Park began turning green with the California-Panama Exposition of 1915. Today, it offers a number of handsome garden installations, including a Rose Garden with more than 2,000 bushes, a tropical setting of cycads and palms, a Desert Garden with a wide array of cacti and succulents, and the formal, fountain-splashed Alcazar Garden, a replication of the gardens of Spain's Alcazar Castle. The lath-sheltered Botanic Building houses an outstanding gathering of tropical and subtropical plants. A sculpture garden and an 1890s carousel are more of the myriad features for the whole family offered by this attraction-filled preserve. In addition to The San Diego Zoo (see below), which the park encompasses, there are a number of theaters, museums, tennis courts, fountains, and picnic areas.

Prickly pear (Opuntia) cacti, among others, inhabit Balboa's Desert Garden.

THE SAN DIEGO ZOO
San Diego

One of the most popular tourist attractions in America, the award-winning San Diego Zoo has been a pioneer in creating indigenous natural habitats, down to the minutest detail, for its animal resident families. This commitment to authenticity for the well-being of its charges, as well as the amenable subtropical climate of its locale, has led the institution to fill over 100

Cushion bush (Cal-ocephalus brownii) in one of The San Diego Zoo's habitats.

acres of tropical forests, mesas, and canyons with a botanic garden's worth of exotic flowering and foliage plants from around the world. Major plant collections assembled over the years include acacias, eucalyptus, fig trees, bananas, aloes, cycads, 40 species of coral trees, close to 1,000 species of orchids, 350 species of palms, 50 species of bamboos, 30 species of gingers, and all kinds of exotic flowering vines to help minimize vertical dividers and enclosures.

A few lions, bears, and wolves remaining from the 1915 Panama-California Exposition celebrating the opening of the Panama Canal marks the genesis of the institution that today boasts over 3,000 mammals, reptiles, and birds, encompassing over 800 species. Three separate out-door amphitheater shows feature live animal performances, and both double-deck bus tours and an aerial tram offer bird's-eye views and relief for tired feet. The Children's Zoo's nursery affords young people the oppor-tunity of meeting newborn animals face-to-face, and its petting paddock allows contact with a variety of hooved animals. One of the zoo's most excitingly realistic exhibits is Tiger River. Opened in 1988, the three-acre Southeast-Asia habitat replica features more than 100 animals in a rain forest of 5,000 plants, made accessible to visitors via a winding pathway simulating a dried river bed. Three hundred high-pressure water nozzles add sultry authenticity by enshrouding the area with mist.

Also operated by the nonprofit San Diego Zoological Society is its 1,800-acre Wild Animal Park located in an undeveloped area inland and 30 miles north of the city. It features a monorail tour of several simulated plains habitats, enabling visitors to observe rhinos, antelopes, deer, giraffes, camels, and other rare species cavorting as freely as they would in the wild. Five different trained animal and bird shows are scheduled every day, and as at the zoo, plantings of exotic flowers of all kinds abound, lending realism to the natural settings.

CONSERVATORY OF FLOWERS
San Francisco

A classic Victorian glass palace that was modeled after the great glass house at Kew Gardens in London, the Conservatory of Flowers has been a Golden Gate Park landmark since the late 1870s. Its perfect jewel-like proportions, though diminutive when compared to, say, the Enid A. Haupt Conservatory at the New York Botanical Garden, are a glorious addition to the park's landscape. A magnificent collection of palms and other tropicals fills the house's central dome and east wing, while its west wing is reserved for spectacular shows of seasonal flowers year-round. I will never forget my first visit to the conservatory and the sight, when I entered this area, of shelf upon shelf of potted cyclamens in intense candy-color reds, pinks, and whites.

Iceland poppies and lofty palms, underplanted with New Zealand flax, pay homage to the lavish Victoriana of Golden Gate Park's Conservatory of Flowers.

The beds of bulbs and annuals that grace the outdoor grounds imme-diately surrounding the conservatory are indicative of this great park's commitment to horticultural finery. In addition to the expansive Strybing Arboretum (see below) and a Japanese Tea Garden, the grounds encom-pass: a Camellia Garden, in full bloom in early spring; a rose garden with 1,000 bushes; a Fuchsia Garden, containing over 3,000 of the marvelous pendulous-bloom plants, in flower from late spring to fall; the 20-acre John McLaren Memorial Rhododendron Dell, bursting with bloom in late spring; and the Queen Wilhelmina Tulip Garden and Windmill.

California poppies (Esch-scholzia) *invite admira-tion at Strybing.*

STRYBING ARBORETUM AND BOTANICAL GARDENS
San Francisco

One of America's great living-plant museums, the Strybing, located within giant Golden Gate Park, was officially opened in May of 1940. As the result of a bequest from Helene Strybing, construction of the 70-acre installation began in 1937 according to the designs of Eric Walther, the arboretum's first director. Early established collections included rare rhododendrons, magnolias, escallonias, and plants originating in Mediterranean-climate regions. The master plan of landscape architect Robert Tetlow in the early 1960s kept the focus on geographic collections ideally suited to the fog-influenced microclimate of coastal northern California: plants from Aus-tralia, New Zealand, South Africa, central Chile, and Asiatic cloud forests.

Thriving with over 5,000 species and designed with great aesthetic appeal, as well as botanical and horticultural merit, the gardens within the grounds include: the Garden of Fragrance; the Eric Walther Memorial Succulent Garden; the Jennie B. Zellerbach Garden, noted for its beds of penstemons and other perennials; the James Noble Conifer Garden; the Moon-Viewing Garden, a Japanese-style landscape; the Biblical Garden; the Takamine Garden, containing Asiatic trees and shrubs; California Native Plants; the Redwood Trail; and the Demonstration Gardens, featuring ideas for the home landscape, including vine arbors with a number of suitable climbers, and a teahouse designed by the famous San Francisco landscape architect Thomas Church.

The institution continually experiments with new species to determine how well they perform in the local climate. Successes are quickly passed on to home gardeners through the arboretum's monthly plant sales. The Helen Crocker Russell Library offers changing art exhibits, as well as some 10,000 book titles and more than 100 periodicals. The grounds are maintained by the Recreation and Parks Department of the City and County of San Francisco. Ongoing development and educational programs are funded through contributions from the Strybing Arboretum Society, a membership-supported, nonprofit corporation founded in 1954.

Beds of bearded iris lend spring enchantment to Overfelt Gardens.

OVERFELT GARDENS
San Jose

A felicitous blend of natural and planted areas, Overfelt Gardens is a restorative and inspiring retreat that the city of San Jose owes to the generosity of the late Mildred Overfelt, a member of one of its pioneer families. Miss Overfelt's parents, William and Mary, purchased 160 acres of land in the 1850s and quickly developed them into a prosperous grain and dairy ranch. An elementary school teacher most of her life, Miss Overfelt deeded 33 choice acres of this land to the City of San Jose in 1959, with the condition that it be made into a public park dedicated to the memory of her parents. The development that followed included the planting of trees, both native and exotic, a Fragrance Garden for the visually impaired, rose and iris beds, annual beds, a Palm Grove, a Camellia Garden, and a fountain. The 25 acres that remained were reserved as a wildlife refuge encompassing three lakes, rolling hills, meandering paths, native oaks, sycamores, alders, and lakeshore plantings of wildflowers and grasses. All kinds of birds and mammals enjoy the attractive habitat throughout the year.

Another interesting and unusual feature of Overfelt is its Chinese Cultural Garden. A celebration of Chinese and American friendship, the five-acre garden displays a number of structures and monuments presented to San Jose by the citizens of Taiwan. These include the Friendship Gate, the Dr. Sun Yat-Sen Memorial Hall and the Chiang Kai-Shek pavilion, all designed in ancient Oriental style by Wang Yu Tang, as well as a 30-foot-tall statue of Confucius overlooking a reflecting pool and an airy, gazebo-like structure called the Plum Pavilion.

A public park since 1966, Overfelt Gardens is maintained and operated by the City of San Jose Department of Recreation, Parks & Community Services.

HUNTINGTON BOTANICAL GARDENS
San Marino

The Huntington is a palatial 207-acre estate, once the home of Henry E. Huntington, a railroad tycoon and real estate developer who loved art, books, and gardens. Established as a cultural and educational institution by Huntington himself in 1919 and opened to the public in 1928, the Huntington ranks today among the nation's great centers of learning. Its library, one of the most complete research facilities in the country, art galleries, numbering the instantly recognizable *Blue Boy* by Gainsborough and *Pinkie* by Lawrence among their staggering collections of eighteenth- and nineteenth-century art, and its 150-acre botanical gardens share a singular devotion to excellence and beauty.

In size and ambition, the grounds merit easy comparison to those of the great houses of Europe. Designed by William Hertrich and begun in 1904, the majestically sweeping landscape of gently rolling lawns accented with statuary, temples, and arbors accommodates 14 specialized gardens. Some emphasize a single family of plants while others are devoted to a particular environment or culture. The most remarkable among the various installations are: the 12-acre Desert Garden, containing the largest outdoor grouping of mature cacti and other succulents in the world; the Japanese Garden, featuring a drum bridge, a Japanese house, a walled Zen garden, and a bonsai court; the Rose Garden, offering a 2,000-year history of the flower and a handsome rose-covered pergola trimmed with latticework; and the Camellia Garden, boasting 1,500 cultivars. Other significant and informative attractions include the Herb, Jungle, Australian, Subtropical, Shakespeare, and Palm Gardens. The vast diversity of plants throughout the gardens coupled with San Marino's auspicious California climate ensures a continuous succession of bloom from January to December.

Each year, more than 30,000 children participate in the Huntington's education programs. The private, nonprofit institution is supported by the generosity of many individuals and groups.

A traditional drum bridge in the Huntington's Japanese Garden is a picturesque foil for aquatic plants and moisture-loving yellow irises.

SAN MATEO JAPANESE GARDEN AND ARBORETUM
San Mateo

Central Park, located in the heart of downtown San Mateo, has long been known for its magnificent old trees, gracious walks, colorful floral displays, and recreational facilities, including a train ride for children. Once the home of Alaska fur trader William H. Kohl, the park—acquired in 1922—is the city's oldest. Two notable features that attract horticultural enthusiasts to the site are its Japanese Garden and its Arboretum.

Opened in 1966 and conceived by Nagao Sakurai, former landscape designer at the Imperial Palace in Tokyo, the Japanese Garden skillfully incorporates views of the park's aged, native oak trees into its traditionally Oriental planting scheme. The shrewd technique lends perspective to the garden and an illusion of spaciousness. Water, plants, and rocks, the three basic elements in any Japanese garden, are cleverly combined here to appear as if untouched by human hands. The "bones" of the garden are evergreen trees, primarily conifers, with variety and interest accomplished by mixing various foliage textures and shades of green. Other kinds of trees, many very rare, lend the setting a feeling of maturity. Flowers relieve the evergreen backdrop with splashes of color, but their presence is understated and subtle. Nonetheless, a surprising variety, including magnolias, flowering cherries, rhododendrons, azaleas, camellias, water lilies, irises, and lotuses, can be seen from late winter through summer.

Adorning the garden throughout are the required ornamental elements, including a teahouse installed in 1968 and a two-ton granite pagoda, a 1966 gift from Toyonaka, Japan, San Mateo's sister city. A pond traversed by enchanting bridges is filled with koi, ceremoniously fed daily at 11 A.M. and 3 P.M. by an attendant in traditional Japanese garb. The garden is administered by the San Mateo Department of Parks and Recreation.

Central Park's Arboretum, founded in 1976, consists of the trees found throughout the park, numbering over 60 species, an All-America Seed Selections Garden, a fern grove, and one of the most extensive collections of Oriental azaleas on the West Coast. Overseeing these installations is The Arboretum Society, sponsor of a garden tour and plant sale every April.

Water lilies brighten a pool at San Mateo Japanese Garden.

HEARST SAN SIMEON STATE HISTORICAL MONUMENT
San Simeon

Arriving at the Hearst Castle Visitor Center for a pre-arranged tour, I admired the gently rolling hills and chaparrals that gradually rose from the coastline. There in the distance atop the highest elevation was a vision that could easily be mistaken for Valhalla. Like a ghostly mirage, La Casa Grande (The Great House), with its 137-foot-tall twin spires, reigns over

Rose standards and soaring Italian cypress, among the army of plants hauled up to the Hearst Castle aerie, conspire to create a sublime setting.

the ocean and the uninhabited coastal plain 1,600 feet below, and bears witness, not to Teutonic gods, but to the outrageous daring and unlimited resourcefulness of one William Randolph Hearst.

William's father, George, a U.S. Senator representing California, purchased a 250,000-acre tract on a remote section of the state's coast in the nineteenth century. On a favorite hilltop, George and his wife, Phoebe, enjoyed entertaining their family and guests with elaborate tented picnics. After the death of his parents, William chose this same site, La Cuesta Encantada (The Enchanted Hill), upon which to erect a palatial estate.

As the owner of a huge publishing empire that employed more than 38,000 people, William Randolph Hearst had enough wealth to indulge his most fantastical whims and aspirations. He began combing Europe for art objects and building fragments, and with the help of Julia Morgan, an architect trained at L'Ecole des Beaux-Arts, he created a showplace that included a 100-room Hispano-Mooresque castle, three guesthouses, pools, terraces, and acres of gardens. Construction began in 1919 and continued unabated until 1947, when ill health forced Mr. Hearst to abandon the isolated site in favor of his home in Los Angeles. He died in 1951, and today, Hearst San Simeon State Historical Monument is meticulously preserved, as it might have appeared in its heyday, by the California Department of Parks and Recreation.

Everything for the vast complex was originally hauled to the site by horse and wagon along a two-mile roadway, uphill all the way. This included tons of soil from the rich bottom lands and full-grown Italian cypress, palms, and native California live oaks for the extensive landscaping. Today, this approach road is lined with oleanders, citrus trees, pomegranates, persimmons, and quinces. The five acres of formal and informal plantings immediately about and around the villa include tree and bush roses, camellias, rhododendrons, annuals, perennials, and assorted groundcovers and flowering vines.

Yucca and barrel cacti make an austere statement at Santa Barbara.

SANTA BARBARA BOTANIC GARDEN
Santa Barbara

The incomparable natural beauty of the coastal community of Santa Barbara is renowned throughout the country, if not the world. The continuing protection of its awe-inspiring canyons and forests amid the foothills of the Santa Ynez Mountains is owed in no small part to the 65-acre preserve permanently set aside as the Santa Barbara Botanic Garden. Mission Canyon, in which the garden is situated, derives its name from the Spanish mission built in the lower canyon in 1786. To meet the water requirements of the area's rapidly increasing population, the mission's Franciscan fathers constructed a dam and aqueduct in 1806 with the help of the Chumash Indians. Sturdily built of local sandstone, the structures survive to this day as an integral part of the northwest portion of the garden.

A botanic garden in Mission Canyon was the idea of Dr. Frederic Clements, a botanist whom many consider to be the father of American plant ecology. With the help of an associate, Dr. Elmer J. Bissell, he succeeded in encouraging Mrs. Anna Blaksley Bliss to purchase the Garden's first 13 acres in 1926. As a memorial to her father, Henry Blaksley, the generous philanthropist established the Blaksley Botanic Garden, to be administered by the nearby Santa Barbara Museum of Natural History, with Dr. Clements as the garden's first director. By 1936, the decision was made to narrow the focus of the preserve to native California plants and to initiate its independence from the museum. A nonprofit corporation under the administration of a board of trustees was formed and from then on, the institution was officially known as the Santa Barbara Botanic Garden.

Revealing spectacular views of the nearby mountains and the Ocean's distant California islands, the garden's trails negotiate arroyos, meadows, canyons, woodlands, a desert area, and a forest of coast redwoods, each with its own plant ecosystem. Major collections include manzanitas (36 species and 30 cultivars), ceanothus (27 species and 34 cultivars), irises (10 species and 77 cultivars), and plants indigenous to the offshore islands. Brilliant yellow California poppies, contrasted with blue-eyed grass, carpet the open areas in spring. Many of the state's rare and endangered plant species are grown in the garden as part of its commitment to conservation.

The information-minded institution houses an herbarium with 86,000 specimens and a library of over 7,000 books. Its Education Department offers classes, lectures, workshops, and field trips for adults as well as children. A nursery stocked with native California plants year-round is staffed by volunteers called Garden Growers who also contribute their time to propagate all of the specimens offered for sale.

UNIVERSITY OF CALIFORNIA AT SANTA CRUZ ARBORETUM
Santa Cruz

Encompassing more than 4,000 varieties of plants, this university-supported installation is well known for having an outstanding collection of plants indigenous to Australia. New Zealand is also well represented as is South Africa, with more than 100 kinds of proteas alone on display. A wide variety of California natives are also on hand at the 80-acre facility, and three greenhouses covering a total of 1,500 square feet, though used primarily for propagation, welcome visitors. Expect to find abundant bloom throughout the grounds from midwinter through June.

*UC Santa Cruz's col-
lection of rare proteas
numbers over 100 kinds.*

HAKONE GARDENS
Saratoga

Nestled on a steep hillside overlooking Saratoga and considered one of the most beautifully authentic Japanese gardens in America, Hakone was originally the 16-acre estate of Oliver and Isabel Stine. Impressed by the Fuji-Hakone National Park during a stay in Japan in 1917, Mrs. Stine named her Saratoga summer residence "Hakone Gardens" upon her return. She enlisted an Imperial gardener to landscape the site in the manner of a seventeenth-century Zen garden and hired a Japanese architect to design two residential structures (the Upper and Lower Houses) appropriate to the setting. Financier Charles Lee Tilden bought the estate in 1932 and added the Mon (main gate). In 1966 he sold the property to the City of Saratoga which acquired the services of the late Tanso Ishihara to maintain the authenticity of the gardens.

The harmonious placement of plants, rocks, and water, the essence of the Japanese style, is in evidence in all four of Hakone's gardens: the Hill and Pond Garden, designed to provide a lovely vista from the upper, or Moon Viewing, House and featuring a waterfall, ponds stocked with koi, a bridge, pavilion, and Mon; the Tea Garden, with stepping stones, a moss garden, a tsukubai (water basin), an ancient Oribe lantern and Tea Ceremony rooms; the Zen, or Dry, Garden, replete with raked gravel, five large stones, black pine, and azaleas; Kizuna-En (the Bamboo Garden), representative of Saratoga's close friendship with its Japanese sister city, Mukoshi, which donated the bamboo fences, stone lanterns, and live bamboo specimens that distinguish this particular garden.

Flowers that enhance the gardens include, in the order of their appearance from December to June, camellias, violets, andromeda, flowering cherries and plums, wisteria, azaleas, irises, peonies, water lilies, and mock orange. The facility is overseen by the City of Saratoga and the Hakone Foundation, a membership organization devoted to the continuing enhancement and authenticity of the gardens.

Azaleas bring spring color to Hakone's raked-gravel Zen Garden.

VILLA MONTALVO ARBORETUM
Saratoga

Dating from 1912, the 3½-acre Villa Montalvo estate is perched in the foothills of the Santa Cruz Mountains, affording sweeping bird's-eye views of the Santa Clara Valley. Set aside in 1942 as a cultural colony where writers, musicians, and artists of every variety could create in quiet harmony with nature, the estate was frequented at one time by scores of celebrated authors and performers. It has been developed into an Audubon Society bird sanctuary as well as an arboretum, containing more than 400 plant species distributed throughout its gently rolling hills. Great old specimen oaks, firs, Italian cypress, and flowering fruit trees embrace formal plantings of rare and exotic flowering species gathered from around the world. A 1½-mile nature trail encounters an abundance of wildlife and more than 60 species of birds in three contrasting California ecosystems: an evergreen forest, a chaparral, and a redwood grove. The Lilian Fontaine Garden Theatre on one of the lawns hosts a variety of concert and theater performances throughout the year. Exhibits of art are staged in an indoor gallery, and the grounds celebrate a show of spring wildflowers every April.

A pair of mute sphinxes and an ancient obelisk guard mounds of feathery gray santolina in bloom in June at Villa Montalvo Arboretum.

PAGEANT OF ROSES GARDEN
Whittier

Designated the most outstanding public rose garden in the nation in 1984 by the All-America Rose Selections, this dazzling profusion of color and scent numbers 7,000 bushes covering more than 600 varieties. Designed by the landscape architecture firm of Cornell, Bridgers and Troller and first opened to the public in 1959, the 3½-acre installation displays a vast diversity of roses, from history's oldest moss rose to the newest introductions and title winners. Paved pathways invite close inspection of 85 beds filled to overflowing with hybrid teas, floribundas, and grandifloras and outlined here and there with delicate miniatures, such as 'Baby Ophelia' and 'Little Fireball'. Climbers are given their due in the Miles of Roses display that lines the fences along Workman Mill Road and Pioneer Boulevard. The more than 500 vining specimens found here represent one of the largest collections of this kind in the world.

Also located within Rose Hills Memorial Park and not to be overlooked is the nearby five-acre Japanese Garden. The traditional landscape's strolling pathways hug the shores of a picturesque lake while encountering a teahouse, bridges, and other ornaments evocative of Eastern mysteries.

An official test site for both the All-America Rose Selections and the American Rose Society, the Rose Garden at Rose Hills dispenses information about the flower and its cultivation at its Visitor Center. A shop on the premises sells plants and floral arrangements, and a variety of special events throughout the year includes a rose care seminar, an amateur photography contest, a children's art festival, and a concert series.

A vast spectrum of varieties, from history's oldest to the newest hybrid teas, grandifloras, and floribundas, populates the Pageant of Roses Garden.

FILOLI
Woodside

One of the most sumptuously beautiful of the great manor houses and gardens built in America in the early 1900s, Filoli (an acronym combining "fidelity," "love," and "life") is a rarity among old California estates in that its original setting remains virtually intact. The outcome of years of loving and meticulous care, the maturity and sheer opulence of its plantings offers a dazzling treat for all devotees of the art of gardening.

California architect Willis Polk designed the mansion with thick, earthquake-proof, red-brick walls for Mr. and Mrs. William B. Bourn II in 1915. Owner of a prosperous gold mine and the nearby Spring Valley Water Company, Mr. Bourn also engaged Bruce Porter to conceive a garden plan for the 16-acre property. With the help of Isabella Worn, Porter came up with a design made up of four distinct areas, or "rooms," in the formal tradition of the great gardens of Europe. With the deaths of Mr. and Mrs. Bourn in 1936, the homestead was acquired by Mr. and Mrs. William P. Roth, who during the almost 40 years of their stewardship, added considerably to the plantings, harmoniously blending the formal with the natural and taking maximum advantage of the surrounding redwood groves and vistas.

The largest of the garden rooms, the Panel Garden, is subdivided into: a rose garden with 500 bushes of 250 varieties in beds edged with box-wood; lavish perennial and annual borders stocked with delphiniums, carnations, purple smoke bush, and yellow poker plant; an orchard under-planted with 20,000 daffodils; and an herbal knot garden. The Woodland Garden room provides a naturalistic canvas for Impressionist splashes of rhododendrons, azaleas, and camellias. The Sunken Garden features the tranquil order of a central water-lily pool and fountain surrounded by lawn, beds of annuals, and formally clipped olive trees. Flowering vines cling to the brick walls of the Walled Garden, enclosing plantings of tulips and annuals and a decorous pavilion designed in Renaissance style by Arthur Brown, Jr., who also designed the nearby Carriage House topped by a handsome columned bell tower. Indebted to the mildness of the ocean-tempered Bay Area's climate, all of the gardens' plantings have been care-fully planned so that visitors will find abundant displays of flowers in every season.

In 1975 Mrs. Roth generously deeded Filoli to the National Trust for Historic Preservation, a nonprofit organization chartered by Congress to help preserve and interpret the historic and cultural elements of America's past. Filoli Center, a nonprofit corporation, was established in 1976 to administer the property in the trust's behalf. The Friends of Filoli, a volunteer support group numbering more than 7,000, provides financial and operational assistance in the maintenance and preservation of the property and sponsors lectures and workshops throughout the year.

A balustrade calls atten-tion to a planting of young wisteria at Filoli.

HAWAII

KAUAI

LAWAI

KALAHEO ●● KOLOA

OAHU

HALEIWA ●
WAHIAWA ● ● KANE ʻOHE
★ HONOLULU

MAUI

KULA ● ● HANA

HAWAII

HILO ●

LILIUOKALANI GARDENS
Hilo, Hawaii

A 30-acre tropical garden with a decided Japanese influence, Liliuokalani began life in 1914 as the idea of Mrs. C. C. Kennedy who was inspired to create a garden after returning to Hilo from a trip to Kyoto. With the aid of her husband, manager of the old Waiakea Mill Company, she succeeded in creating a setting of stone lanterns, bridges, pagodas, and footpaths amid native plantings that included coconut palms and mangoes. After being washed away by a tidal wave that struck Hilo in 1946, the garden was rehabilitated by the County Parks Department with funds appropriated by the Hawaiian legislature. Today, the setting presents a lively and unique juxtaposition of exotic tropical plants and old lava ledges with Japanese structural elements, including a moon bridge, lion gates, a torii, and a teahouse donated by the Urasanke Tea Ceremony Foundation of Kyoto. Though originally a swamp in parts and having no shortage of ponds, the park features a traditional Japanese dry garden designed by noted land-scape artist Nagao Sakurai and containing rocks, ferns, bonsai, and white sand representing a mountain stream.

A grand old conifer towers over a pond at Liliuokalani Gardens.

NANI MAU GARDENS
Hilo, Hawaii

On the big island of Hawaii in the shadow of the Mauna Kea Volcano, this people-oriented display garden presents the exotic flora of south seas paradises in all their lush and vibrant beauty. Founded in 1970 by Makoto Nitahara on 20 acres of the undeveloped Panaewa rain forest atop lava flows from nearby Mauna Loa, the property was initially cleared to make room for a commercial papaya field. By 1973, approximately 100 varieties of fruit trees, plus red and blue jade vines, bougainvillea, hibiscus, orchids, and heliconias had been planted. By 1978, the Orchid Garden, comprising 2,000 varieties in a 150-by-25-foot pavilion, as well as Ginger and Anthurium Gardens were completed, establishing the site as a showcase for the major commercial plants of the "Big Island" and as a tropical botanical garden befitting the name, Nani Mau, meaning "forever beautiful" in Hawaiian.

Beds of red salvia and other annuals contribute to the spectacular, crowd-pleasing displays that are a specialty of Nani Mau Gardens.

The garden's present owner, Seiichi Sorimachi, purchased the facility in 1987 and added annual flower beds, an artificial waterway, four gazebos, and a greenhouse for the propagation of orchids. In the style popular at Disneyland (see p. 22) and numerous Canadian display gardens, bedding plants at Nani Mau spell out "Aloha" and "Hilo Hawaii" and depict the Hawaiian cape and helmut symbol. A cascading waterfall, ponds filled with carp and water lilies, a fern forest, a Hawaiian herb garden, and more than 100 tropical fruit and nut trees round out the 17 acres' horticultural treasures.

OLA PUA BOTANICAL GARDEN AND PLANTATION
Kalaheo, Kauai

Once part of the estate, built in 1932, of the plantation manager for the Kauai Pineapple Company, this 12-acre garden features a collection of over 4,000 native and introduced subtropical and tropical fruits, flowers, and trees. Principal subdivisions of the verdant tropical setting include: the Jungle, where shaded paths encounter swamp mahogany and other trees heavy with anthuriums, bromeliads, and vanilla orchids; an outstanding collection of hibiscus hybrids; the Palm Garden; and the Kua Kua (food) Garden, where tropical fruit trees surround a picnic area. Other plants abundantly represented include aroids, heliconias, calatheas, gingers, cacti and succulents, and water lilies.

Birds of paradise are among the flocks of exotic flowering species that glow amid the sultry tropical habitats of Ola Pua Botanical Garden.

MOIR'S GARDENS
Koloa, Kauai

One of the world's most outstanding collections of cacti and African aloes may be found at a resort hotel on Poipu Beach called Kiahanu Plantation. The gardens, filled with exotic dryland plants and tropicals, are the labor of love of Sandie Moir, who along with her husband received the plantation as a wedding gift. The ocean-viewing grounds also include a coconut grove, a stand of taros, tumbling waterfalls, and ponds alive with water lilies and Japanese carp. The setting is enhanced by a sprinkling of interesting antiques and artifacts.

*The incandescent beauty
of tropical water lilies
awaits at Moir's Gardens.*

NATIONAL TROPICAL BOTANICAL GARDEN
Lawai, Kauai

Chartered by Congress to create a national resource in tropical botany and officially dedicated in 1971, this 185-acre botanical garden is devoted to scientific research and education. Located in the Lawai Valley, an area of great natural beauty, the garden is in the process of developing its collections, including: plants of nutritional and medicinal value; rare and endangered species in need of conservation; tropical fruits and spices; and palms, erythrinas, gingers, and other ornamentals. The facility fulfills the long-felt need for a tropical research garden within the United States at a time when vast numbers of undescribed and unstudied species are rapidly being destroyed.

*Giant water lily pads,
among the many
wondrous curiosities at
National.*

Also at the same site are the 100-acre Allerton Gardens, the former estate of the late Robert Allerton whose generous financial support helped make the National Tropical Garden a reality. A setting of tranquil beauty that was originally created by Queen Emma in the 1870s and greatly expanded by Allerton and his son, John, the gardens feature statuary and other ornamental elements and a wide array of flowering tropicals.

The Botanical Garden's commitment to education is reflected in its Professional Gardener's Training Program for high-school graduates and its Internship Program for college and university students interested in practical gardening experience. An active publishing program emphasizes the scientific, but a number of titles of interest to the amateur gardener are available by mail. Though congressionally chartered, the garden is a private institution supported by contributions and membership.

Heliconia, an exotic Hawaiian native likely to be encountered at Kahanu.

KAHANU GARDENS
Hana, Maui

This lushly beautiful setting, a 120-acre botanical treasure nestled along the rugged black lava coast of Maui's eastern shore, emphasizes plants traditionally used by the Polynesians. These early settlers of the Hawaiian Islands brought with them many of the ethnobotanicals (plants relied upon for everyday food, shelter, or medicine) now growing at Kahanu. Distinctive among these collections are a pandanus (screw pine) forest and more than 20 varieties each of coconut and breadfruit from throughout the tropical regions of the world. The garden's walking trail affords appreciation of a vast assortment of tropical fruits, nuts, and root crops, as well as a sacred ancient temple, Piilanihale Heiau, named for the first reigning family of the Maui kingdom. It was these people's descendents, along with the Hana Ranch, Inc., who gave the preserve its first 60 acres of land in 1973. Kahanu Gardens is owned and maintained by the congressionally chartered National Tropical Botanical Garden (see p. 78).

KULA BOTANICAL GARDENS
Kula, Maui

Hugging the slopes of near two-mile-high Haleakala Crater, this 14-acre eden is animated by running streams and cascading waterfalls. Featuring a wide range of native Hawaiian plants on land owned in the nineteenth century by Princess Kekaulike, once the governor of the island of Kauai, the lush, naturalistic setting was established in 1971 by Warren I. McCord, a landscape architect from California. Development continued for more than two years before the site was opened to the public in April of 1971.

A garden at Kula Botanical sports red poinsettia bracts in late autumn.

Paths wander along the streams, under arbors and over a covered bridge, and reveal incomparable vistas of the Central Valley, the West Maui Mountains, Maalaea and Kahului bays, and the distant islands of Lanai and Molokai. An impressive collection of proteas, natives of South Africa, attests to the fact that the South Pacific is one of the few areas of the world where these enigmatic, otherworldly blooms can be grown successfully. A tabu garden displaying various poisonous plants, an aviary with white doves, peafowl, and pheasants, a koi pond, and a fern grotto are some more of the many features that attract visitors to this exotic setting year-round.

WAIMEA FALLS PARK ARBORETUM AND BOTANICAL GARDENS
Haleiwa, Oahu

Spread across an 1,800-acre valley, Waimea Falls Park offers an abundance of the virgin tropical splendor one expects to encounter in Hawaii, but fears is fast succumbing to encroaching development. Within the park, the Waimea Arboretum and Botanical Gardens offer a vast collection of more than 5,000 kinds of plants, many of them listed as endangered species. Among the more than 30 garden subdivisions encountered along the facilities' wandering, hibiscus-bedecked trails are: the Lei Garden, planted with plumerias and other flowers customarily used in the making of the familiar Hawaiian garlands; the Palm Meadow, filled with examples from various parts of the Hawaiian Islands; the Malaysian Garden, containing more than 100 varieties of the large-leaved plants indigenous to the tropical Asian country; the unique Hibiscus Evolutionary Garden, with wild species and modern hybrids tracing the history of Hawaii's state flower; the Heliconia Garden, containing examples as tall as 20 feet; the Ginger Garden, one of the largest collections of its kind in the world; and the Ethnobotanical Garden, offering the plants the early Hawaiians relied on for food, medicine, clothing, shelter, and utensils.

A spectacular cascading waterfall and river-size stream add their splendor to the preserve, as does a colorful variety of wild and domesticated birds. Entertainment for the whole family is offered in the form of hula dances, Hawaiian games, and diving exhibitions. Both open-air tram tours for the weary or walking tours for the energetic are scheduled regularly.

A pool at Waimea Falls Park, alive with a variety of tropical aquatics, is indicative of the preserve's many horticultural splendors.

FOSTER BOTANIC GARDEN
Honolulu, Oahu

Nestled in the heart of downtown Honolulu, this extraordinary 20-acre preserve contains a wide selection of botanic examples, some native to Hawaii, others from distant lands. The larger among its collections are palms, plumerias, bromeliads (1,400 species, 50 genera), orchids (over 10,000 plants representing both wild species and modern hybrids), and mature and unusual trees from all over the globe. There are displays devoted to poisonous plants and dye plants, and the Prehistoric Glen, planted in 1965 by the Garden Club of Honolulu, features primitive plants whose fossil remains have given us many modern-day fuels and medicines.

The garden can trace its roots to 1850 when Queen Kalama sold the land to William Hillebrand, a German doctor who produced the botanic milestone, *Flora of the Hawaiian Islands*, and planted many of the towering trees flourishing in the garden today. Before returning to Germany in 1867, he sold the acreage to Capt. and Mrs. Thomas Foster who continued its development until 1930 when the site was bequeathed to the City of Honolulu. Named the first director of the garden, Dr. Harold Lyon introduced 10,000 new kinds of trees and plants over a span of 27 years and started the orchid collection with his own personal acquisitions.

Owned and maintained by the City of Honolulu Department of Parks and Recreation, the garden sponsors a thriving program of courses and field trips for both children and adults. The Friends of Foster Garden, with membership open to all, both near and far, provides financial and volunteer support for the garden's various activities.

Bamboos are among the broad spectrum of exotic trees at Foster Botanic.

The brilliant red of Hawaiian ti is in abundance at Lyon Arboretum.

HAROLD L. LYON ARBORETUM
Honolulu, Oahu

A living laboratory for university and community college classes as well as for elementary and secondary schools, the Harold L. Lyon Arboretum is a 124-acre facility of the University of Hawaii at Manoa. Encouraging and facilitating research, instruction, and public service related to its unique resources, the preserve was established in 1918 by the Hawaiian Sugar Planters' Association Experiment Station to demonstrate the restoration of rain forest vegetation, to test trees for reforestation, and to collect plants of economic value. It was presented to the University of Hawaii in 1953.

Encompassing greenhouses, a nursery, and an herbarium, the lush grounds display more than 4,000 species of plants, including collections of palms, ficus, taro clones, aroids, gingers, heliconias, marantas, gesneriads, ornamental ti, vireya rhododendrons, and native and endemic Hawaiian flora. Publishing a wide variety of books and pamphlets related to tropical plants and endangered species, the institution also sponsors a full schedule of courses, workshops, and outings for professionals and nonprofessionals of all ages. An annual plant sale is held every August, and the Garden Club of Honolulu, Hawaii Bromeliad Society, and American Orchid Society meet regularly on the premises, which also serve as a germ-plasm depository for the Heliconia Society International.

MOANALUA GARDENS
Honolulu, Oahu

A tropical paradise in the Kamananui Valley once owned by Princess Bernice Pauahi Bishop was inherited in 1884 by Samuel Mills Damon, who developed the grounds as they are today. Interesting historic structures dating from before Damon's time survive in a setting of native Hawaiian species, including kukui, bamboo, banyan trees, taro, hala, and koa. A stream and a pond stocked with koi add a welcome note of water to the lush greenery. The garden regularly schedules educational programs for children and field trips for young and old alike. The grounds are the site of the Prince Lot Hula Festival, held every year on the third Saturday of July. Fun for the whole family, it features arts and crafts demonstrations, hula dances, and Hawaiian games.

The graceful branches of a monkeypod tree reach out over an expanse of lawn at Moanalua Gardens, a repository of a vast number of native species.

QUEEN EMMA SUMMER PALACE
Honolulu, Oahu

Listed on the National Register of Historic Places and housing a museum of Hawaiian history, this lush, three-acre estate in the Nuuanu Valley is named for the wife of King Kamehameha IV, Hawaii's nineteenth-century ruler. The Queen commissioned the celebrated Dutch landscape architect Augustus de Holstein to design the garden for her summer residence, and he obliged by filling the grounds largely with roses, geraniums, and lilies. The garden today displays many of de Holstein's and Queen Emma's preferences, including a fascinating collection of delicate spider lilies, in full bloom in late spring. Trees on the property number many mature specimens that the Queen herself planted, and complementing the flower gardens are a variety of native Hawaiian species, including the candlenut tree and the Loulu palm.

Polypodium ferns and a blooming ginger in fall at Queen Emma Summer Palace.

HO'OMALUHIA
Kane'ohe, Oahu

Originally designed and constructed by the U.S. Army Corps of Engineers to provide flood control for the city of Kane'ohe, Ho'omaluhia is a 400-acre natural forest preserve filled with fascinating flowering and fruiting trees, shrubs, and vines. While special emphasis has been placed on preserving and increasing plants unique to Hawaii, the garden has also been equipped with species, many rare and endangered, from various tropical regions of the world, representing a rich source of learning and enjoyment for visitors of all ages. Camping facilities and hiking and horseback-riding trails have been thoughtfully provided, and guided nature walks and environmentally related programs and classes are scheduled throughout the year for young and old alike. A number of streams and a 32-acre lake add to the site's already magnificent natural splendor. Like Wahiawa (see p. 86) and Foster (see p. 82), Ho'omaluhia is one of the Honolulu Botanic Gardens, owned and maintained by the Honolulu Department of Parks and Recreation. It was opened to the public in 1982.

The untamed magnificence of Oahu's terrain is on view at Ho'omaluhia.

WAHIAWA BOTANIC GARDEN
Wahiawa, Oahu

Located on the cool 1,000-foot-high plateau between the island of Oahu's two main mountain ranges, this lush garden preserve occupies a site that was once used by the Hawaii Sugar Planters' Association for forestry experiments. The sun-dappled, thickly forested garden fills a 27-acre gulch with flowering and fruiting plants from throughout the world. These include such trees as allspice, cinnamon, chicle, Indian mahogany, and the Chinese soap nut and camphor, and such exotic fruit species as the earpod and the Red River fig. The entrance walk of the garden is adorned with mulesfoot and Australian tree ferns, and its main terrace boasts trees over 60 years old. Major collections include gingers, aroids, hibiscus, heliconias, calatheas, and palms (including the traveler's from Madagascar, so named, legend has it, because of the quart of water stored in the base of each of its giant leaves). Wahiawa Botanic Garden is cultivated and maintained by the City of Honolulu Department of Parks and Recreation.

A monumental Mindanao gum, one of the many great old trees awaiting deference at Wahiawa Botanic.

OREGON

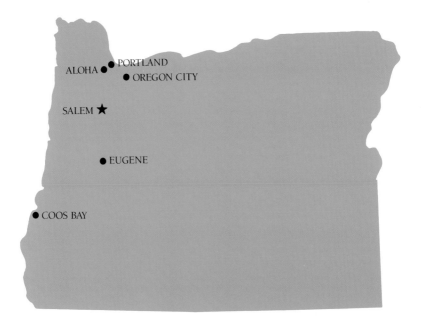

JENKINS ESTATE
Aloha

A hunting-lodge–style main house, built by Ralph and Belle Ainsworth Jenkins in 1913, and its surrounding 68 acres of grounds, establishes the rustic mood of this country gentleman's estate. Stables, a carriage house, greenhouse, pump house, water tower, teahouse, and 1880s farmhouse are set off by expansive lawns and formal gardens that include generous perennial beds and rhododendron displays.

The traditional English-style gardens were lovingly developed over the years by Mr. and Mrs. Jenkins, but from the time of Belle Jenkins's death in 1963 until 1975 when the site was purchased by the Tualatin Hills Park & Recreation District, the gardens suffered from terrible neglect. Thanks to the efforts of the district, with the help of various local garden clubs and societies, the grounds were restored to their former splendor. Today, in addition to the formal plantings, pathways winding throughout the estate give access to a rock garden, lilacs, and broad carpets of wildflowers that are alive with color in spring. Rare and exotic shrubs and trees from all parts of the world help to make the facility, listed in the National Registry of Historic Places, an inspiration to gardeners.

Fragrant lilac is among the shrub blooms that beautify Jenkins Estate.

SHORE ACRES STATE PARK GARDEN
Coos Bay

High above the crashing surf of Oregon's rugged coastline southwest of Coos Bay, a trio of state parks offers access to the area's natural splendor to thousands of visitors each year. Sunset Bay, Cape Arago, and Shore Acres

Geometric beds trimmed with boxwood at Shore Acres State Park Garden are the result of the restoration of designs first laid out in the early 1900s.

parks share spectacular vistas of the craggy shoreline, and the last boasts a sparkling jewel of a garden nestled among its towering Douglas firs and Monterey cypress.

Shore Acres was once the 743-acre estate of lumber baron Louis J. Simpson who purchased the tract in 1905, and as a Christmas present for his wife, began the construction of a palatial summer home on it in 1906. A three-story edifice containing an indoor heated swimming pool and spacious ballroom at completion, the house was matched in its grandeur by the gardens that were eventually carved out of the surrounding country-side. These included geometrically laid out, boxwood-trimmed formal beds, expanses of meticulously manicured lawn, and a Japanese garden built around a 100-foot-long oval lily pond. Plying the Pacific rim with Oregon timber, the captains of Simpson's ships brought back exotic plant varieties that were added to the gardens as well as introduced to the commercial nurseries springing up at the time along the West Coast. At one point Simpson employed five full-time gardeners to care for flower beds bordered by 2,000 feet of boxwood and hawthorn hedges.

Destroyed by fire in 1921, the original mansion was replaced by an even larger one, but Simpson's timber empire began to crumble in the 1930s, and no longer able to afford the upkeep of Shore Acres, he sold it to the Oregon State Parks Division in 1942. Having deteriorated beyond repair, the mansion was razed and the grounds were left to ruin until a major restoration effort was begun in 1971. The result of painstaking detective work completed in 1975, the formal gardens in evidence today follow the original layout. Boxwood-bordered beds abound with hydrangeas, roses, dahlias, bulbs, annuals, perennials, and many of the same exotics that graced the originals. The Oriental garden as well may now be appreciated in all its former glory.

Where the mansions once stood, on a bluff overlooking the turbulent sea, a glass-enclosed observation post shields visitors from drenching sprays as they enjoy a 180-degree panorama of the picturesque coastline.

Species and hybrid rhododendrons, as well as evergreen and deciduous azaleas, parade their bloom from January to August at Greer Gardens.

GREER GARDENS
Eugene

For a natural setting containing the largest collection of rhododendrons in the United States, Greer Gardens is the place to visit. The installation was begun in the mid-1960s by Harold E. Greer, with the help of his father, for the sheer pleasure of assembling and displaying a wide variety of these prolific bloomers. After the death of the elder Greer in 1972 and a terrible freeze that destroyed most of the plants the same year, Harold restarted the four-acre garden and established a nursery business specializing in rhododendron and azalea hybrids and other rare trees and shrubs, vines, and groundcovers.

In addition to the nine acres now devoted to the nursery, where plants for sale are displayed in neatly organized rows, the original ornamental garden offers spectacular, mature examples of all kinds of species and hybrid rhododendrons (blooming in a range from January to August, depending on variety) and both deciduous and evergreen azaleas. Many of the hybrids, such as R. 'Trude Webster', were developed by Greer.

HENDRICK'S PARK RHODODENDRON GARDEN
Eugene

A tribute to the initial efforts in 1951 of the Eugene chapter of the American Rhododendron Society, this ten-acre installation contains an amazing 5,000 rhododendrons and azaleas, a sight to behold in full bloom in the spring. Accenting the major display are viburnums, magnolias (40 varieties), dogwoods, and witch hazels, and contained within the remainder of Hendrick's Park are a number of towering Douglas firs of impressive age. Meandering paths across lawns and under Oregon white oaks afford scenic views of the surrounding countryside.

The magnolia cultivar 'Picture' in glorious bloom at Hendrick's Rhododendron Garden, where a variety of flowering trees accompany the main display.

THE MOUNT PISGAH ARBORETUM
Eugene

A bucolic 118-acre nature preserve alive with all the myriad flora and fauna that the great Pacific Northwest wilderness embraces is what awaits the visitor to this remarkable setting. A self-guiding, one-mile nature trail, created by the Friends of Mount Pisgah Arboretum with special consideration for children, exposes young and old alike to the intricate ecologies of the marsh, stream, forest, and meadow.

The native marvels of Mt. Pisgah include translucent dogwood leaves.

Among the wonders that unfold along the trail are: the Intermittent Stream, carrying water on its way to the Pacific from the upper reaches of 1,520-foot Mt. Pisgah, its banks lined by a stand of Oregon ash (*Fraxinus latifolia*), a moisture-loving tree early settlers enlisted for making furniture and farm implements; the Oak Savanna, a meadow scattered with large Oregon white oaks (*Quercus garryana*), their branches dotted with the round galls that the larva of tiny wasps engender and grow in; the Mossy Rock, demonstrating how mosses and lichens break down rock into soil that can support more evolved plants; the Douglas Fir Forest, showing how the signature tree of the Northwest naturally prunes itself of its lower branches as its growing crown shades out the sun; the Upper Plateau, an open meadow where the thin soil exposes patches of rock but manages to sustain the enchanting Pacific native dogwood (*Cornus nuttallii*); the Seasonal Marsh, dry in summer but wet and boggy in spring, when it blooms with the yellow monkey flower (*Mimulus guttatus*); the South-Facing Hillside, its small oak trees festooned with fishnet lichen; and finally, Incense Cedars (*Calocedrus decurrens*), a stand of towering conifers whose aromatic resins perfume the air along the last section of the trail.

The arboretum hosts an Arbor Week celebration (in April), a Wildflower Show (in May), a Mushroom Show (in October), as well as an Outdoor School for thousands of Lane County children each year and a number of other educational workshops and programs. Supported almost entirely by private donations and volunteers, the nonprofit institution is working toward building a collection of the world's woody plant species, to be arranged in a series of groves, each representing one of the world's major habitats.

OWEN ROSE GARDEN
Eugene

Containing 4,500 bushes representing 100 old-fashioned as well as hybrid-tea varieties, this 5-acre All-America Selections garden is picturesquely located along Eugene's Willamette River. Enhancing the formal and informal rose plantings are beds of Japanese iris that were given to Eugene by its sister city, Kakegawa, Japan. Also witnessing the scene in silence is the Black Republican cherry tree, Oregon's oldest, dating from the 1860s. It blooms in early April; the roses are at their peak in mid-June.

Radiant hybrids like the Scotch rose join old favorites at Owen.

JOHN INSKEEP ENVIRONMENTAL LEARNING CENTER
Oregon City

This enchanting installation is proof positive that wildlife habitats can survive in the heart of urban environments. Once the drainage facilities and parking lots of a Smucker's berry processing plant, eight acres of hills, ponds, and creeks have been reclaimed and redeveloped into an arboretum that serves as a facility for explaining ecological interactions. In various demonstrations, ideas are presented for environmentally sound and energy-conserving gardening and landscaping, yard-debris composting, solar-heated greenhouse growing, plastic recycling, and other practices that are attracting the interest of conscientious gardeners.

Also enlightening among the features of the Learning Center are a Birds of Prey exhibit, salmon and trout production installations, and the Haggart Memorial Observatory, housing the second largest telescope in the Northwest.

Garden-debris composting is illuminated at John Inskeep Learning Center.

THE BERRY BOTANIC GARDEN
Portland

The Berry Botanic Garden affords an intimate appreciation of the Pacific Northwest's forest canopy, with its majestic Douglas firs and other stately trees indigenous to the coastline west of the Cascades. This handsome preserve comprises a species garden, a facility for botanical research and study, and a display garden featuring woodland, streamside, and rock-garden habitats.

Rhododendrons, dwarf conifers, alpines, and perennials supply a rockery at The Berry Botanic Garden with copious bloom in April.

In the 1930s, a renowned plantswoman, Mrs. A.C.U. Berry, began collecting plants from all over the world for her heavily wooded southwest Portland property. As a supporter of plant hunting expeditions to China and Tibet, she was the recipient of rare seed, much of which yielded the more than 1,000 rhododendrons found in the garden today. These, along with other favorite plants, such as alpines and primulas, formed the basis of her collection. After her death in 1976, the future of her outstanding achievement was secured by the formation of the Friends of Rae Selling Berry Botanic Garden.

Officially incorporated in 1978, the garden is one of nineteen botanical institutions comprising the Center for Plant Conservation, an organization dedicated to education and research concerning America's endangered plants. The garden's commitment in this regard is demonstrated by the fact that it maintains a cryogenic bank for seeds of various threatened species.

CRYSTAL SPRINGS RHODODENDRON GARDEN
Portland

Seven acres of rhododendron species and hybrids in glorious bloom in April and May are the feature attraction at the Crystal Springs Rhododendron Garden. The sound of a cascading waterfall in the Jane Martin Entrance Garden welcomes visitors to spring-fed Crystal Springs Lake, where in addition to rhododendrons, companion plantings of ferns, azaleas, dogwoods, Japanese maples, alpine species, and others abound. Completing the atmosphere of natural largess is the huge waterfowl population that finds the lake and its surround an ideal habitat.

Established in 1950 by the American Rhododendron Society as a facility for testing rhododendrons, the garden is part of the city of Portland park system. The broad diversity of its plantings and its naturalized beauty make it a pleasurable and informative experience throughout the year.

Azaleas, as well as rhododendrons, adorn Crystal Springs Lake.

THE GROTTO
Portland

Father Ambrose Mayer, a priest of the Order of the Servants of Mary, came to Portland in the early 1920s with the dream of establishing a shrine to the mother of Jesus. The 62 acres of rocky woodland and cliffs he purchased as the site for his sanctuary inspired the building of The Grotto, a cavern 30 feet wide and deep and more than 50 feet high cut into the face of a 110-foot-high cliff, with an altar hewn out of its interior rock. Completed in 1925, this natural cathedral, surrounded by towering fir trees and housing a marble replica of Michelangelo's *Pietà*, has become a peaceful place of worship and renewal for more than 100,000 visitors every year.

Atop the cliff, reached via a ten-story elevator, the grounds of the Servite friars' monastery are graced by a rose garden, a sunken garden, beds of ferns, annuals, and perennials, and a series of reflection ponds. The near-at-hand natural beauty of the setting is matched by the breathtaking views it affords of southwest Washington State, including the Columbia River and Mt. St. Helens. The statuary and smaller shrines that punctuate the landscape of the two-level sanctuary are made all the more inspiring by the wonders of nature that embrace them.

An annual Christmas festival of lights features a number of family-oriented activities, including puppet shows and a petting zoo.

Cinnamon ferns, among other kinds, grace The Grotto's monastery.

Magnolias contribute their sensuous bloom to Hoyt Arboretum.

HOYT ARBORETUM
Portland

The 175-acre Hoyt Arboretum contains tree and shrub species collected from all parts of the world. Established in 1928 and owned by the city of Portland, the acreage boasts the country's largest assemblage of conifers. Included among these are examples of Brewer's weeping spruce, Himalayan spruce, dawn redwood, Chinese lacebark pine, and a grove of coast and giant redwoods. Also represented are oaks, maples, and magnolias.

With spectacular cityscape and mountain views in the distance, ten miles of gently winding paths invite the visitor to take in the show of flowering shrubs, trees, and native wildflowers, in performance from mid-March through June. Brilliant foliage color, along with wild mushrooms, beckons in autumn. Bristlecone Pine Trail insures an opportunity for the disabled to view the arboretum's extensive collections.

INTERNATIONAL ROSE TEST GARDEN AT WASHINGTON PARK
Portland

Roses, roses everywhere might be the catchphrase of this spectacular display located in 332-acre Washington Park, part of Portland's eight continuous miles of west hills parks. Ten thousand bushes representing 400 varieties adorn terraces high above the "City of Roses," with views of Mt. Hood and other peaks of the Cascades in the distance.

The oldest public rose test garden in the United States, the four-and-a-half acres of formal beds were established in 1917 to evaluate selections of roses for color, fragrance, disease resistance, and other characteristics.

Established in 1917, the International Rose Test Garden is the oldest facility of its kind in the United States; 10,000 bushes fill four-and-a-half acres.

With the support of civic-minded citizens and The American Rose Society, the installation was founded in 1917 by Jesse A. Currey, who became its first curator. One of 24 official testing sites for the All-America Rose Selections (an organization of commercial rose growers and hybridizers established in 1940), the garden is also one of four testing grounds for miniature roses, under the auspices of the American Rose Society.

Rose aficionados of every ilk will find something to please them, from the latest hybrid teas and miniatures in elevated beds to old-fashioned varieties, in this remarkable collection. Peak bloom months are June, July, August, and September. Also to be found in the immediate vicinity are The Japanese Garden (see below) and an informal Shakespeare garden with walkways amid trees, annuals, and perennials.

THE JAPANESE GARDEN AT WASHINGTON PARK
Portland

In Washington Park, within a stone's throw of the International Rose Test Garden (see p. 97), is a superlative Japanese-style garden. Designed by P. Takuma and executed by P. T. Tono, the installation was opened to the public in 1967, and although covering only 5½ acres, it succeeds in the illusion that it goes on forever. The climate of the Pacific Northwest, similar to Japan's, has helped make this garden one of the finest of its kind in North America.

Divided into five sections, each an example of a particular type of Japanese garden, the whole serves up a rich sampling of the elements characteristic of Japan's ancient, symbolic approach to garden design. In the Flat Garden, where plants are used sparingly, rocks and raked gravel predominate. The Natural Garden provides a pathway that wends its way among native trees and shrubs, waterfalls, and streams. In the Strolling Pond Garden, the largest of all, ponds, waterfalls, and an abundance of plantings, including cloud-pruned trees, are organized into an evocatively picturesque landscape. An elaborate teahouse imported from Japan is the centerpiece of the Tea Garden. Especially memorable to me were the ingeniously woven bamboo fences and gateways found throughout the gardens.

Artfully conceived bamboo dividers are among the ornamental elements that imbue Washington Park's Japanese Garden with a decidedly Oriental mystique.

LEACH BOTANICAL GARDEN
Portland

In a woodland hollow carved by Johnson Creek, this nine-acre garden, with over 1,000 species and cultivars, focuses on plants native to the Pacific Northwest. Additional collections include winter bloomers, witch hazels, ferns, native iris species, groundcovers, and deciduous azaleas from the eastern United States. Much of the facility is organized according to rock garden, woodland, bog, and streamside habitats.

Lilla Leach, an accomplished botanist, with her husband John, a pharmacist and community leader, explored the Northwest in the 1920s and '30s in search of ornamentally noteworthy native species. Among Mrs. Leach's most outstanding discoveries are *Kalmiopsis leachiana*, a small rhododendron-like plant, and a native yellow iris, *Iris innominata*. The five-acre garden the Leaches created in the 1930s was an expression of their devotion to each other, as well as the environment they investigated. In

1979 they donated their estate to the city of Portland, and in 1981, through Leach Garden Friends, with the assistance of the Portland Bureau of Parks and Recreation, it became Portland's first public botanical garden. Four additional acres were acquired in 1984.

From streamside plantings through cool woodlands to open meadow uplands, the garden is a collage of ever-changing colors, textures, and sounds. The Leach's manor house, with its handsome wood detailing, stands guard over winter blooms, berries, and fruits in February, spring blossoms from March through May, and annuals throughout the summer.

Enkianthus campanulatus *supplies brilliant fall color to an inviting woodland setting at Leach Botanical, where natural habitats bloom all year.*

WASHINGTON

THE BLOEDEL RESERVE
Bainbridge Island

Once the home of the Bloedel family, which remains responsible for its continued development, Bloedel Reserve encompasses 150 inspiring acres, 84 of which are forested with trees typical of the Pacific Northwest. The remainder of the grounds, evolving over a period of 35 years, is beautifully landscaped with formal and informal plantings, ponds, and meadows. Major points of interest include: the Glen, where, in late spring and early summer, rhododendrons flower under the protection of second-growth timber, and perennials, bulbs, wildflowers, and more than 15,000 cyclamen plants fill the naturalized setting with color during the rest of the blooming season; the Japanese Garden, featuring the elements of stone, sand, and a guest house combining traditional Japanese-teahouse and Pacific Northwest Native-Indian-longhouse designs; the Moss Garden, with its living green carpet complemented by huckleberries and protected by a canopy of the large leaves of Hercules walking stick trees; and the Reflection Garden, dominated by the geometric precision of a rectangular reflecting pool. The Visitor Center, occupying the former manor house of the estate, is graced by a formal, European-style landscape that includes lakes, swans, weeping willows, Dutch elms, a parrot tree, and a magnificent pair of empress trees. A Bird Refuge, wildlife habitats, and woods abounding with Douglas fir, western red cedar, hemlock, and lush undergrowths of ferns and other native species complete the sylvan splendor of this extraordinary site.

The Reserve is operated under the auspices of the Arbor Fund, which interprets and extends the vision of the Bloedel family.

Rhododendrons pack the Glen at The Bloedel with voluptuous bloom.

Charmingly arranged plantings of herbs of all kinds with flowering plants make The Herbfarm an inspiring and informative attraction all year.

THE HERBFARM
Fall City

Begun in 1974 by Lola and Bill Zimmerman, this commercial enterprise has grown into a delightful attraction that celebrates the herb in all of its endlessly useful expressions. Located in a suburb of Seattle, the farm compound includes 17 theme gardens, demonstrating suggested planting designs and illuminating various facets of herbal lore and history. The Pioneer Garden, for example, contains varieties deemed essential for culinary and medicinal purposes by the early settlers who trekked west on the Oregon Trail. The various gardens feature herbs of all kinds—from common parsley and chives to such exotics as scented geraniums, lemon verbena, and anise hyssop (a minty plant with edible flowers)—interplanted in many instances with spring bulbs, perennials, and annuals to attractive and inspiring effect.

The nursery on the premises offers a selection of 250,000 plants, representing 639 different kinds of herbs and perennials, from May through September, with a somewhat reduced inventory from October through April. More than 250 classes and workshops scheduled from April through Christmas are devoted to herb-related horticulture, crafts, and cooking, and a restaurant on the site specializes in gourmet offerings of herb-seasoned dishes.

All of this would seem to be more than enough to stimulate the imaginations of the most inveterate of herb fanciers, but the Herbfarm issues twice-yearly, sampler-style catalogues presenting a panoply of mail-order seeds and herbal products, and celebrates a variety of festivals, fairs, and special events from Mother's Day in the spring to just before Halloween in the fall.

THE RHODODENDRON SPECIES FOUNDATION
Federal Way

The preservation, distribution, and display of age-old species rhodo-dendrons (not modern cultivars) is the noble pursuit of this conscientious organization. Its 24-acre botanical garden boasts 1,800 forms of approx-imately 500 species, the largest collection in existence of these wild and seductive flowering plants. Examples from all over the world, including Britain, Japan, Korea, and Taiwan, are displayed with native and intro-duced companion plants in a handsomely designed woodland setting. Features of the installation include: a 2½-acre study garden that affords easy comparisons of the various kinds of rhododendrons; an alpine gar-den, re-creating a Himalayan mountain scree with the kinds of rhodo-dendrons and other plants that survive the rigors of high altitudes; a pond garden; an impressive collection of Japanese maples; and a gazebo made entirely from a single cedar log. Ensuring an extended show, early-, mid-, and late-blooming varieties of the rhododendrons flower in March, April, and May, respectively.

Founded in Eugene, Oregon, in 1964 by Dr. Milton V. Walker and a small group of American Rhododendron Society members, the RSF was begun in an effort to develop a comprehensive collection of species. The first acquisitions were planted in Dr. Walker's garden. But through a gen-erous offer by the Weyerhaeuser Company, the installation was moved in 1974 to its present site on the grounds of Weyerhaeuser's corporate head-quarters in Federal Way. Also to be found at this location is the one-acre Pacific Rim Bonsai Collection. Opened to the public in 1989 and adminis-tered by the RSF, this facility contains 50 outstanding bonsai examples from Taiwan, China, Japan, and the United States.

The Rhododendron Species' alpine garden evokes a Himalayan mountain habitat.

State Capitol Conservatory, shown in June, boasts blooming plants all year.

STATE CAPITOL CONSERVATORY
Olympia

Built in 1939 as a WPA endeavor, this 16,000 square-foot glass house was once used to grow cut flowers and plants for offices throughout the capitol campus. Now open to the public and hosting thousands of visitors annually, the facility displays more than 500 tropical and desert plants, as well as seasonally flowering varieties. Christmas marks the installation of over 200 poinsettias in six different colors, and throughout the rest of the year, a show of bloom of some kind can be counted on. The conservatory also witnesses the start of many of the annuals that populate the colorful beds throughout the capitol grounds in summer. Other flowering assets outdoors include bulbs and cherry trees in spring and hundreds of roses and thousands of perennials in summer. The conservatory is operated under the direction of the Department of General Administration's Office of Campus and Community Services.

CHILDREN'S HOSPITAL & MEDICAL CENTER
Seattle

Providing welcome comfort and diversion for patients, staff, and visitors, a collection of distinguished gardens covers 12 acres of the 25-acre central campus of this Seattle health-care institution. Begun in the 1950s and expanded in the mid-1970s as part of a major building program, the gardens are supported by on-site nursery and greenhouse facilities where plants are propagated and tested for inclusion in the landscape. The grounds' diverse collection encompasses an amazing 1,750 kinds of plants dispersed throughout various installations, including: a mixed perennial border, linking the hospital entrance with the parking garage and featuring an impressive assortment of herbaceous choices interplanted with woody specimens that add structure to the design; a heather garden, where the foliage and bloom of heaths, heathers, and other ericaceous plants create constantly changing patterns of color and texture throughout the year; and a stand of Akebono cherry trees (*Prunus yedoensis* 'Akebono'), bordering the hospital's entrance drive and greeting arriving patients with a spectacular display of bloom during the first week of April.

Children's Hospital & Medical Center is a nonprofit, private pediatric institution serving Washington, Alaska, Montana, and Idaho.

Spiky blue salvia and pink dianthus cheer the Children's Hospital gardens.

CARL S. ENGLISH, JR., GARDENS
Seattle

A celebration of bloom offered by dogwoods, cherries, magnolias, crab apples, rhododendrons, and azaleas in late spring distinguishes this remarkable seven-acre garden. Located along the fascinating Hiram M. Chittenden Locks joining Lakes Union and Washington with Puget Sound, this installation, featuring more than 1,000 plants of international origin, was developed by Carl S. English, Jr., a plant explorer who gathered specimens from all over the world from 1933 to 1974. Major collections, in addition to those named above, include oaks, ginkgoes, maples, and heathers. A number of unusual specimen trees, including Chinese witch hazels and stewartias, dot the grounds in tandem with a series of seasonal flower beds. Built by the Army Corps of Engineers in 1916, the eight-mile-long locks feature visitor displays explaining the installation's function and purpose. Investigation of the locks and the gardens provides an enlightening and entertaining outing for the whole family.

Rose arbors at the English Gardens attractively tame climbers in June.

JAPANESE GARDEN OF WASHINGTON PARK ARBORETUM
Seattle

The Alaska-Yukon-Pacific Exposition of 1909 exposed Seattle to the mysteries of the East and whetted its appetite for an authentic Japanese-style garden. But it was not until well after the Washington Park Arboretum (see p. 108) had been established in the 1930s that the dream began to come to fruition. An anonymous gift from a member of the Arboretum Foundation set the wheels in motion in 1957, and Juki Iida, designer and builder of more than 1,000 Japanese gardens worldwide, was chosen to direct the project. Arriving from Japan in 1960, he personally selected more than 500 boulders, ranging from 1,000 pounds to 11 tons, from the Cascade Mountains and carefully placed them at the 3½-acre site. Around these, thousands of plants were arranged to represent a variety of settings typical of those found in Japan. The specimens chosen include hundreds of azaleas and rhododendrons, as well as camellias, evergreens, flowering trees, mosses, and ferns.

The garden's original teahouse arrived in Seattle as 1,500 pieces packed in 14 crates, a gift from the people of Tokyo. After being destroyed by fire in 1973, it was rebuilt according to its initial design and given the name "Arbor of the Murmuring Pines." A hedge composed of osmanthus, boxwood, and cedar encloses the area immediately around the teahouse, creating a garden within the greater garden of streams, ponds, conifers, water lilies, Japanese iris, maples, and cherries. Gates, a pagoda, a wisteria arbor, bridges, and contemplation shelters further the restful Oriental atmosphere. A crowning touch, sitting high on a knoll, is the 200-year-old Kobe Lantern, 3½ tons of granite, hand-carved and a gift from the citizens of Kobe, Japan.

For most of its existence, the garden was managed by the University of Washington as part of the arboretum. In 1981 its management and operation was transferred to the Seattle Department of Parks and Recreation.

Pendulous wisteria blossoms frame the spring bloom of viburnums and azaleas at Washington Park Arboretum's Japanese Garden.

WASHINGTON PARK ARBORETUM
Seattle

On 200 acres stretching south from Lake Washington's Union Bay is an extraordinary collection of woody plants, a living reference of 5,500 kinds that thrive in the mild Puget Sound climate. The majestic woodland setting nurtures hundreds of varieties of maples, camellias, lilacs, hollies, and rhododendrons and major displays of magnolias, cherries, and conifers. Northwest natives mingle with species indigenous to Europe, Asia, New Zealand, Australia, South America, Africa, and the eastern United States.

Outstanding installations include: Azalea Way, a three-quarter-mile-long path lined with flowering cherries, azaleas, and dogwoods, in bloom from March to June; Loderi Valley, where large-leaved and Loderi hybrid rhododendrons, flowering in May, are sheltered by March- and April-flowering magnolias; Rhododendron Glen, where species and hybrids, ranging from dwarfs to tree forms, flower from early March to midsummer; Winter Garden, featuring plants that bloom between October and March, including witch hazels and viburnums, with special attention to the striking combination of the bare stems of *Cornus mas* underplanted with Lenten roses; Foster Island, a wildlife sanctuary in which pines, oaks, and birches have been introduced; and Woodland Garden, where a large collection of Japanese maples flourishes in a shaded valley. A first-class Japanese Garden (see p. 107) is also contained within the grounds.

The arboretum was started, and is still funded, jointly by the University of Washington and the City of Seattle. The prestigious Olmsted Brothers landscaping firm developed a master plan in 1936, and many features of that design remain today. State and federal work-relief programs built the original trails, roads, and buildings. Donations from private individuals and groups, such as the Arboretum Foundation and the Seattle Garden Club, continue to provide crucial support.

Washington Park Arboretum glows with brilliant color in October. The site's master plan was first laid out by the firm of Olmsted Brothers.

WOODLAND PARK ZOOLOGICAL GARDENS
Seattle

An aviary encompassing a huge tropical forest and other naturalized settings of tropical and subtropical plants are among the features that make this remarkable collection of over 1,000 animals an attraction for flora, as well as fauna, fanciers.

Woodland Park began when Guy Phinney, a leading Seattle real estate developer, purchased a 188-acre tract near the south shores of Green Lake for his personal estate, and called it Woodland Park in honor of its stands of towering cedars. In addition to a magnificent mansion, Phinney installed formal gardens and a private zoo containing deer, ostriches, raccoons, and a bear. And he encouraged the general public to visit his menagerie. After his death in 1883, the city of Seattle purchased the estate and hired the famous Olmsted Brothers to develop a public park, incorporating the formal gardens and Phinney's animal collection.

Officially established in 1904, the zoo today harbors 1,000 animals in various habitats, each with appropriate indigenous plantings: an award-winning five-acre African Savanna, a mountain landscape for snow leopards, an indoor nocturnal house, a wetlands for birds and reptiles of the marsh and swamp, and an Asian Elephant Forest, among others.

Woodland Park also contains within its environs a formal rose garden. Established in 1922 and boasting more then 5,000 plants of 200 varieties, it is an official test site for All-America Rose Selections.

Conifer topiaries stand like sentinels over Woodland Park Zoological Gardens' formal rose garden, an official All-America Selections site.

MANITO PARK CONSERVATORY AND GARDENS
Spokane

Part of a park system among the many designed by Olmsted Brothers of Brookline, Massachusetts, for various American cities, Manito Park is one of those rare exceptions that features extensive floral gardens and a conservatory. Development of its 90 acres commenced under the supervision of the city Park Board in 1907. By 1913 most of its recreational facilities, its present-day conservatory—home to a gathering of tropicals and renamed in memory of park patron Dr. David Gaiser—and Duncan Garden had been completed. This last, covering a three-acre expanse, was designed by John W. Duncan in French-parterre style, with an elaborate central fountain surrounded by symmetrically placed beds of annuals, in bloom all summer. Since 1913 a number of outstanding horticultural attractions have been added.

The unique abundance of the English-style perennial border, with its vast diversity of textures, colors, and flower types, may be appreciated in the Joel E. Ferris Perennial Garden. Flowering in the three-acre display begins in spring with bulbs and primroses, and ends in fall with chrysanthemums.

A cooperative effort between the Spokane Rose Society and Park Department, four-acre Rose Hill features formal beds of 1,500 bushes, over 150 varieties of kinds available to the general public. At another site nearby, informal beds and borders are planted with old-fashioned favorites.

The Nishinomiya Garden, named in honor of Spokane's sister city in Japan, is a classic example of Japanese-style landscaping. Designed by Nagao Sakurai and opened in 1974, the installation is an artful blending of flowering shrubs and trees, rocks, a waterfall, a pond, a bridge, a contemplation shelter, and stone lanterns. Other horticultural attractions at the park include the Lilac Garden and a rock-wall garden.

A rock-wall garden at Manito Park tumbles with basket-of-gold alyssum, purple arabis, pink phlox, and white perennial candytuft (Iberis).

POINT DEFIANCE PARK
Tacoma

On a promontory jutting into Puget Sound and surrounded by spectacular distant mountain vistas, this 700-acre park features seven gardens of note. The Rose Garden contains hundreds of rose bushes, including several

Point Defiance Park's Japanese meditation garden blooms serenely in June with yellow irises, a white Oriental dogwood, and a single doronicum flower.

trained on arbors. The Japanese Garden's tranquil setting features a number of suggested meditation points. The 100-year-old Annual Display Garden is inhabited by more than 60,000 flowering plants every year. The Rhododendron Garden comprises a natural setting featuring a diversity of varieties. The Dahlia Test Garden offers hundreds of new cultivars for inspection before introduction on the market. The Camellia Garden contains over 100 plants, and the Native Garden offers five habitat ecosystems: an eastern cascade, a coastal forest, a subalpine setting, a bog region, and a high alpine and scree environment. The park's remaining acreage encompasses untouched forests and woodlands and a variety of recreational attractions, including a beach, a zoo, and an aquarium.

W. W. SEYMOUR BOTANICAL CONSERVATORY
Tacoma

Dating from 1908 and one of only three Victorian-style conservatories on the West Coast, the Seymour is located in Tacoma's Wright Park and is listed on the City, State, and National Historic Registers. The remarkable structure, dominated by an impressive 12-sided central dome, is made up of more than 12,000 panes of glass. Its permanent displays contain 200 species of exotic tropicals, including ornamental figs, fruit trees, birds-of-paradise, orchids, cacti, and bromeliads. A waterfall and a pool with colorful goldfish are favorite attractions of younger visitors.

Named in honor of William W. Seymour, a utilities, lumber, and land baron who funded its construction in 1907, the facility was rebuilt in 1937, under the auspices of the WPA, and restored again in 1956 and

1976. With the help of various local garden and community clubs, a number of changing displays are staged throughout the year. These include an Easter celebration of bulbs, azaleas, rhododendrons, and lilies, a poinsettia spectacular at Christmas, an array of annuals and perennials in summer, along with an outdoor offering of All-America Selections award-winning annuals. Chrysanthemums populate the space in fall and a pumpkin festival for children is held in October. The conservatory is owned and operated by the Metropolitan Park District of Tacoma.

Tropical species numbering more than 200 are sheltered in the Seymour Conservatory, one of the country's oldest glass houses, dating from 1908.

OHME GARDENS
Wenatchee

Ohme Gardens is the 60-year handiwork of a single family bent on turning an arid, rocky mountainside into an emerald green, Alpine-picture-book setting. In 1929 Herman Ohme and his new bride, Ruth, took ownership of 40 acres of land that included a high bluff with sweeping views of the Wenatchee Valley, the Columbia River, and the Cascade Mountains. With an eye toward creating a simple, quiet retreat for themselves, the Ohmes began digging up small evergreens from the surrounding mountains and hauling them in a car to their aerie property. Over the years, these numbered into the thousands, and were joined by hundreds of tons of rock that the Ohmes arranged by hand to form pathways, pools, and borders for lawns and plantings.

Spurred by the enthusiasm of occasional visitors, the couple opened the site to the public in 1939. After Herman's death in 1971, Ruth continued contributing to the care of the garden, but it was her son, Gordon, who assumed full responsibility for its development, continuing the work he had begun at his father's side. Through his efforts, the reclamation grew to its present nine acres.

Seemingly untouched by human hands, the setting could have been lifted right out of the picturesque Bavarian Alps. Trees, low growing alpine plants, groundcovers, stone, and water combine to evoke the kind of high mountain country where beauty is not dependent on floral display. Craggy rock outcroppings emerge from carpet-like plantings of creeping phlox and thyme, sedums, vinca minor, and mosses. Stone Pathways wander across patches of sod and alpine meadow, past rustic shelters, ever upward until reaching the bluff's highest point, where a stone lookout affords the best view of the surrounding mountainscape.

Sedum and thyme blooms add color to Ohme Gardens' sumptuous panoramas.

CANADA

BRITISH COLUMBIA

● NORTH VANCOUVER
VANCOUVER ●
● ROSEDALE
VICTORIA ★ RICHMOND

⅄ PARK & TILFORD GARDENS
North Vancouver

Miraculously, eight distinct gardens pleasantly fit into the compact 2½ acres that make up this city oasis. Established in 1969 by Schenley Canada, Inc. (then called Canadian Park & Tilford Distilleries Ltd.) as a gift to the people of North Vancouver, the gardens were designed as a community beautification project by the landscape architects Justice and Webb on an abandoned lot adjacent to the distilleries. The carefully planned placements of trees, shrubs, water, and rock were a popular attraction until 1984 when the distillery shut down and the plantings fell into severe decline. In 1987 the BCE Development Corporation acquired the property and determined to restore it along the lines of its original outdoor-room concept. Undertaken by the firm of Durante Kreuk Ltd., the work was completed and presented to the public in 1988.

One of the many assets of this installation is that every one of its theme gardens, by nature of its manageable size and scope, is a ready-reference source of inspiration for the city or suburban home garden planner. Abounding with easily adaptable ideas and cleverly separated from each other by hedges and screens are: the formal Rose Garden, with rose, clematis, and honeysuckle vines covering brick-pillared arbors, and brick-edged beds filled with rose bushes; the Herb Garden, planted with all kinds of medicinal and culinary favorites; the Flower Gardens, where three changing displays of bulbs and annuals each year are contained within shrubbery borders; the Colonnade Garden, its arches hung with baskets of fuchsias, its beds overflowing with hostas and ferns; the Rhododendron Garden, a south-facing bank filled with rhododendrons and azaleas

Lupines, acidanthera, and daisies glow in Park & Tilford's White Garden.

shaded by pines, magnolias, and dogwoods; the White Garden, with an abundance of white-flowering perennials, annuals, and shrubs; the Oriental Garden, with a moon-gate entrance, an arching bridge, and a reflecting pool where koi dart among water-lily pads; and a Native Garden, where a brook gurgles among rocks, ferns, and wild grasses, and thickets of thimbleberry and devil's club grow under a canopy of hemlocks, cedars, maples, and Douglas firs.

Thousands of tulips participate in Fantasy Garden World's spring display.

FANTASY GARDEN WORLD
Richmond

What was once called Bota Gardens, a six-acre installation developed by John Massot and opened in 1980, has been transformed into a fantasyland showplace devoted to the delight of children as well as adults. Responsible for the expansion of the property to its present 21 acres are Bill and Lillian Vander Zalm who purchased the original gardens in 1984. The succession of crowd-pleasing features added to the site since then attests to the fertile imagination and personal vision of Mrs. Vander Zalm. These include: a 23-bell carillon imported from Holland; an old-fashioned conservatory for tropical plants and catered events; a rose garden with a gazebo/teahouse; arbors hung with baskets of fuchsias and begonias; an Oriental garden; and no less than six exotic-bird aviaries.

A garden specifically designated for children encompasses a farm-animal petting zoo, a duck pond, Noah's ark, and rides that include a miniature train. The Fantasy European Village, a complex of more than 20 shops and restaurants staffed with appropriately costumed workers, offers the wares and cultures of faraway lands.

Throughout the grounds are vibrantly colored beds of bulbs and annuals and ponds stocked with water lilies. Ten acres of formal gardens include a

Biblical Garden featuring life-size statuary. The crowning addition to the complex is the replica of Holland's Coevorden Castle, which the Vander Zalms transported aboard a barge from its original location in downtown Vancouver to its present site at the gardens. The castle and other buildings and the grounds' trees are bedecked with thousands of lights during the Christmas season.

RICHMOND NATURE PARK
Richmond

If you ever wondered where that gardening staple, sphagnum moss, comes from, Richmond Nature Park holds the answer and much more. At this 105-acre natural bogland and forest, an educational adventure for the whole family, the moss may be observed growing in a protected natural habitat, of which there are all too few in North America. Boardwalks over the boglands and winding trails through the forests introduce visitors to all kinds of native plant life, including shore pine, labrador tea shrub, bog blueberry, and the tiny insectivorous sundew. The natural preserve attracts a variety of feathered wildlife, including hummingbirds, red-tailed hawks, Canada geese, and the fabled great horned owl. Children will especially enjoy the "Rabbitat," an enclosed area inhabited by furry species native to the locale, and the Nature House, containing several hands-on exhibits, live animals, and a working beehive. The park's own publications, addressing environmental and conservation topics, may be purchased at the site.

Bog laurel (Kalmia po-liifolia), *among the bloom found at Richmond Park.*

The Canadian maple leaf, in begonias and dusty miller at Minter Gardens.

MINTER GARDENS
Rosedale

Carpeting the base of 7,000-feet Mt. Cheam with 27 acres of color, the densely planted vivid bloom of this enchanting site is organized according to various themes. These include a Stream Garden, a Lake Garden, a Meadow Garden, a Fern Garden, a Fragrance Garden, a Rose Garden, an Alpine Garden, a Formal Garden, an Arbor Garden, and a Rhododendron Garden distinguished by a cooling waterfall tumbling in tiers amid the blossoms. The veritable kaleidoscope of color is intensified by ornate Victorian-style flower beds and hoop-skirted topiary "Southern Belles" made entirely of blossoms. Azaleas, annuals (one of the largest displays in Canada), perennials, and profusions of hanging baskets add their own distinctive charm to the festivities, while streams, ponds, a nature trail, a maze, aviaries, and a petting zoo promise amusement for the whole family.

Horticulturist Brian Minter and his wife, Faye, owners of the gardens, accidentally happened upon a picturesque old farm site on a family outing in 1977. Recognizing the potential of the rocky terrain, with its spectacular mountain scenery, the couple set about developing it into a show garden. The realization of their dream was opened to the public in 1980, and has been attracting tens of thousands of visitors annually ever since.

✳ BLOEDEL CONSERVATORY
Vancouver

Once a stone quarry, Queen Elizabeth Park is a sylvan city retreat offering recreational activities, landscaped gardens, a Civic Arboretum with extensive collections of native, as well as foreign, species, a planetarium, and, most notably, the Bloedel Conservatory. Like a vision of the future, this 70-foot-high triodetic dome rises from a terrace of pools and fountains, with the North Shore Mountains providing a spectacular backdrop. Constructed of 1,490 triangular Plexiglas bubbles, the Buck Rogers–like structure spans a diameter of 140 feet to cover 15,386 square feet of tropical and desert plantings traversed by bridges and walkways.

Seasonal floral displays, towering palms, pools swimming with koi, a waterfall, cacti and succulents, exotic blooms, and free-flying tropical birds find refuge in the warm sanctuary the year round. It was officially dedicated on December 6, 1969, by His Worship, Mayor T. J. Campbell, and Mrs. Prentice Bloedel, and is administered by Vancouver's Board of Parks and Public Recreation.

Bloedel's dome rises above a Japanese-style garden at Elizabeth Park.

STANLEY PARK
Vancouver

A partially forested preserve of nearly 1,000 acres, Stanley Park is set on a peninsula that juts north into Burrard Inlet. A six-mile road tracing the site's periphery commands breathtaking views of the sea, woodlands, mountains, and city skyline. Two hundred acres of the park are devoted to a dizzying array of recreational facilities, probably unmatched by any other city park, including beaches, tennis courts, a golf course, an aquarium, and a zoo. Thousands of migrating birds, trumpeter swans and Canada geese among them, make use of the setting as well. Horticultural standouts number the Rose Garden, with 3,500 bushes encompassing 80 varieties, and the perennial beds, filled to overflowing from spring to fall with an enormous variety of bloom.

A covered bridge brings old New England charm to Stanley Park.

DR. SUN YAT-SEN CLASSICAL CHINESE GARDEN
Vancouver

The first authentic, full-scale garden of its kind ever constructed outside of China, this enchanting installation, named in honor of the Republic of China's first president, is modeled after private gardens developed in the city of Suzhou during the Ming Dynasty (1368–1644). Reflecting the Taoist philosophy of yin and yang, the skillful design is a balance of light and dark, hard and soft, and small and large. The four basic elements essential to the traditional Chinese garden are all present and accounted for in this compact, one-third-of-an-acre landscape: structures, including pavilions, covered walkways, terraces, and lookout platforms; rocks, functioning both as sculpture and as the "natural" elements of a suggested rugged terrain; water, in the form of tranquil pools and gentle streams, representing the yin principle of quiet reflection; and plantings, symbolic of human virtues. The garden's pine, bamboo, and winter-blooming plum, for example, known as the Three Winter Friends, celebrate strength, grace, and the renewal of life, respectively.

The tranquil, meditative setting in the heart of bustling Vancouver represents the cooperative effort of more than 50 experts from the city of Suzhou in China, under the leadership of master architects Wan Zu-Xin and Fen Xiao Lin, working with the architect Joe Wai and the landscaper Don Vaughan, both of Vancouver. All of the non-plant components, including rocks and pebbles, were shipped from China in more than 950 crates. Construction began in March of 1985, and the garden was officially opened in April of 1986. Funding was provided by the government of Canada, the Chinese province of Jaingsu and city of Suzhou, and by private endowment and donations.

Bamboos at the Dr. Sun Yat-Sen Garden symbolize the human virtue, grace.

UNIVERSITY OF BRITISH COLUMBIA
BOTANICAL GARDEN
Vancouver

This 75-acre installation, established in 1916 and the oldest university botanical garden in Canada, is set like a shining jewel amid the dark green of the expansive coastal forest preserve on Vancouver's western peninsula. Beautifully designed and organized, its ten theme gardens include the following:

The E. H. Lohbrunner Alpine Garden, occupying 2½ acres, constitutes a massive rockery display of mountain flora from around the world. Organized according to the continent from which each originates are edelweiss, blue gentians, wild orchids, and trilliums, among others.

The eight-acre Native Garden features extensive trails winding through a variety of the province's natural habitats: woodland and meadow, peat bog, and brook and pond. Indigenous plants along the way include devil's club, dogwoods, sage brush, and a native cactus from British Columbia's dryland interior.

Plants from the famous Chelsea Physic Garden in England form the nucleus of the herb collection in the UBC Physick Garden. Herbaceous plants typically grown in the sixteenth century to cure the ills of the body are displayed in formal beds centered on a sundial.

A large latticework pavilion, forming an impressive centerpiece for the entire grounds, is adorned with hanging baskets and a variety of climbing plants suited to the Vancouver climate. The nearby Food Garden offers grape vines, berry bushes, and fruit trees espaliered in traditional fashion.

The 30-acre Asian Garden, the largest of the subdivisions, encompasses a magnificent collection of exotic magnolias, species rhododendrons, and

Hydrangea blooms accent October foliage color at UBC Botanical Garden.

climbing roses and other vines. These are surrounded by drifts of blue Himalayan poppies and beds of nodding primulas.

The Nitobe Memorial Garden is a 2½-acre authentic Japanese garden created in 1960 by Dr. Kannosuke Mori. Clouds of cherry blossoms hover throughout in spring, and brilliant foliage color paints the area in autumn. Other major displays at the UBC Botanical Garden include the Contemporary Garden, the Pinetum, the Winter Garden, and the Alpine Cool House.

Providing an extensive and diverse educational program among its many activities, the garden receives operating and endowment support from The Davidson Club, a membership organization established in 1982.

VANDUSEN BOTANICAL GARDEN
Vancouver

Affording impressive views of the nearby coast range mountains, this 55-acre garden retreat is nestled in the geographic center of Vancouver. Its gently undulating landscape is a pleasantly flowing sequence of distinct gardens and plant collections punctuated by ponds, rock outcroppings, sculpture, and broad expanses of lawn.

The enormous variety of plants displayed is arranged according to both geographic origins and botanical relationships. The former, representing various locales around the world, include: the Sino-Himalayan Garden, with Oriental poppies, rare magnolias, liriodendrons, davidias, maples, and 200 species of Chinese or Himalayan rhododendrons; the Eastern North America Collection, displaying deciduous trees, conifers, shrubs, and wildflowers native to the eastern part of the continent; the Mediterranean Garden and Cedrus Collection, with plants common to the dry, rocky hillsides of the Mediterranean region, including herbaceous perennials, bulbs such as allium (flowering onion), the strawberry tree (*Arbutus unedo*), Russian olive, and various species of cedar, including the magnificent cedar of Lebanon (*Cedrus libani*); the Southern Hemisphere Collection, with plants from South America, New Zealand, Australia, and Tasmania, including the curious monkey puzzle tree (*Araucaria araucana*) and species of senecio, olearia, and hebe, ornamental shrubs from New Zealand; and the Western North America Flora collection, with pines, junipers, spruces, firs, azaleas, lilies, triliums, and irises indigenous to the Pacific Northwest.

Major related-plant collections located throughout the grounds are heathers, perennials, groundcovers, ornamental grasses, hydrangeas, rhododendrons, camellias, Japanese azaleas, dwarf conifers, hollies, viburnums, magnolias, and plants of the Rose Family. A formal rose garden, a children's garden, a maze made with 1,000 pyramidal cedars (*Thuja occidentalis*), totem poles, a rock garden, and 11 stone sculptures carved at their sites are more of the garden's memorable features. An imaginatively conceived building nestled into a hillside, MacMillan Bloedel Place, houses a theater and hands-on exhibits devoted to the intricacies of the forest ecosystem.

Development of VanDusen began in 1971 when its three major contributors, the Government of British Columbia, the City of Vancouver, and the Vancouver Foundation signed an agreement to provide funds for the creation of a botanical garden. The landscaping of the site and the management of the institution were entrusted to the Vancouver Board of Parks and Recreation. Named for the late W. J. VanDusen, president of the Vancouver Foundation and instrumental in the development of the province's lumber industry, the garden opened to the public in 1975.

Summer bloom animates a VanDusen Botanical Garden rockery stream.

THE BUTCHART GARDENS
Victoria

Butchart is synonymous with color. Very few public gardens in North America can compete with its vividly rainbow-hued flower beds, achieved by periodically replacing plants so that peak perfection is constantly maintained.

The history of the 50-acre garden began when Mr. and Mrs. Robert Pim Butchart purchased a 130-acre tract of land and built a house on it in 1904. Mr. Butchart, a pioneering manufacturer of Portland cement in Canada, was the president of a nearby processing plant, and Mrs. Butchart immediately began developing the grounds of their estate, which they named Benvenuto. A particularly unsightly abandoned limestone quarry on the property presented a problem that Mrs. Butchart eventually surmounted by creating a sunken garden. Densely planted with a colorful selection of annuals, biennials, perennials, and flowering shrubs, and partially flooded to create a pool and waterfall, it has been one of the most spectacular attractions at the gardens since they were opened to the public more than a half century ago.

The Butchart Italian garden's ornateness is abetted by lily pools.

The Butcharts gradually expanded the facility over the years, adding plants they collected on their world travels each winter. Numbered among the colorful installations to be enjoyed today are the Rose Garden, the Japanese Garden, the Italian Garden, with formal water-lily pools, and Mrs. Butchart's Private Garden, a symphony of white latticework and cascading pink geraniums in summer. Magnificent displays of rhododendrons, azaleas, tulips, poppies, schizanthus (butterfly flower), primroses, and begonias blanket the grounds seasonally, and all of the plantings are illuminated at nightfall.

Mr. and Mrs. Butchart died in 1943 and 1950, respectively. Privately owned by their heirs, the gardens are managed by one of their grandchildren, R. Ian Ross.

FABLE COTTAGE ESTATE
Victoria

A visit to this 3½-acre dazzling array of color is not unlike stepping onto the set of Munchkinland in the film version of "The Wizard of Oz." A treat for children especially, the sheer volume of flowers arranged in fantasy settings, the storybook props, and animated figures invite one to leave the real world behind and enter the realm of the imagination. This is what Bernie Rogers did when he conceived and built the oceanfront cottage that dominates the site. Taking 11 years to build, it features a simulated thatched roof made of individually molded shingles held in place with more than 600 pounds of glue. The unique structure attracted hordes of the curious, and no longer able to enjoy any privacy, the Rogers family sold their dream house in 1969, with the understanding that both the exterior and interior, with its rounded surfaces and hand-hewn furniture, would be kept intact for all to enjoy.

A profusion of bloom of all kinds distinguishes Fable Cottage Estate and completes the fairy-tale atmosphere that children find irresistible.

Taking the hint from the cottage, the development of the grounds continued the storybook theme. Nine Wishing Gardens, each with its own exuberant floral design and animated figures, depict various wishes for the visitor. A winding path along a stream opens into the Floral Valley Gardens, memorable for their spectacular display of giant tuberous begonias from May to October. Other delights of the grounds include wheelbarrows and cornucopias spilling over with mounds of flowers, a "Ship of Your Dreams," carrying a cargo of bloom as it "sails" across a lawn, and giant hanging baskets trailing flowers by the armful.

HATLEY PARK—ROYAL ROADS MILITARY COLLEGE
Victoria

Opulent splendor typical of the many great estates that blossomed in North America at the turn of the century shows itself unabashedly at Hatley Park. Built in 1908 by James Dunsmuir, a coal and railroad tycoon and Lieutenant-Governor of British Columbia (1906–1909), Hatley Castle is a fortress in stone, 200 feet in length, with a turret soaring 82 feet over 650 acres of grounds. Dunsmuir died in 1920, and his widow remained at the estate until her death in 1937. Purchased by the Canadian government in 1940, the complex continues to house the Royal Roads Military College, commissioned as an officer training establishment that same year.

The vast grounds of Hatley Park were laid out by the Boston landscaping firm of Brett and Hall, and are maintained today in a manner befitting their intended grandeur. Great old trees, pastures, ponds, and an orchard alternate with three principal gardens. The formal Italian Garden, with original urns, statuary, and a graceful curving pergola, is planted with clematis, climbing roses, phlox, an 80-year-old wisteria, delphiniums, and boxwood hedges. The four-acre Japanese Garden contains three lakes, a teahouse, copper beeches, Western red cedars, rhododendrons, and Japanese maples, cherries, and umbrella pines. A naturalized garden, patterned after those popular in eighteenth-century England, hugs the shores of a lagoon, providing sanctuary for flocks of birds. Also to be found on the grounds are greenhouses and a rose garden.

Crab apple blossoms frame the teahouse at Hatley's Japanese garden.

VISITORS' INFORMATION

KEY TO SYMBOLS

Brochures	Gift shop
Parking	Guided tours
Labels	Visitors' center
Picnic facilities	Membership
Restaurant	Courses

THE UNITED STATES

ALASKA

THE GARDENS AT THE MUSEUM OF ALASKA TRANSPORTATION AND INDUSTRY
P.O. Box 909   Palmer, AK 99645
(907) 745-4493 ▪P✗🍴GT 🎟 ⤴

Directions	Palmer is a small community located in south central Alaska, about 40 mi. northeast of Anchorage.
Hours	Tuesday through Saturday 8 A.M. to 4 P.M.
Admission	Fee charged.
Wheelchair access	Throughout.
Special features	Transportation and industry exhibits, of special interest for children.

CALIFORNIA

DISNEYLAND
1313 Harbor Boulevard   Anaheim, CA 92803
(714) 999-4000 ▯P♇⏛✕⛫GT

Directions	From Los Angeles, take Hwy. 5 south to Harbor Blvd. south; entrance is well marked.
Hours	Every day 8 A.M. to 1 A.M. during summer months; 10 A.M. to 6 P.M. weekdays and 9 A.M. to midnight on weekends during winter months.
Admission	Fee charged.
Wheelchair access	Throughout.
Special features	Rides and attractions of all kinds for adults and children.

LOS ANGELES STATE AND COUNTY ARBORETUM
301 North Baldwin Avenue   Arcadia, CA 91006-2697
(818) 446-8251 ▯P♇⏛✕⛫GT⊘▣♪

Directions	Located in Arcadia, 15 mi. northeast of downtown Los Angeles.
Hours	Arboretum, every day 9 A.M. to 5 P.M.; closed Christmas Day; gift shop, every day 10 A.M. to 4 P.M.; narrated tram tours (extra fee) run in afternoon on weekdays, 10:45 A.M. to 4 P.M. on weekends; guided tours of Santa Anita Depot, Tuesday and Wednesday 10 A.M. to 4 P.M.
Admission	Fee charged; no fee for children age 4 and under.
Wheelchair access	Throughout.
Special features	Reference library; herbarium; historic restorations.

BERKELEY ROSE GARDEN
Department of Parks   201 University Avenue   Berkeley, CA 94720
(415) 644-6530 P♇⏛

Directions	Located about 1 mi. north of the UC campus, at the intersection of Euclid Ave. and Bayview Pl.
Hours	Every day, dawn to dusk.
Admission	No fee.
Wheelchair access	Throughout.

BLAKE GARDEN
University of California   Berkeley, CA 94720
(415) 524-2449 ▌P ♉ ⚓ GT

Directions	Located at 70 Rincon Rd. in Kensington.
Hours	Monday through Friday 8 A.M. to 4:30 P.M.
Admission	No fee.
Wheelchair access	Throughout.
Special features	Estate restoration.

REGIONAL PARKS BOTANIC GARDEN
Tilden Regional Park   Berkeley, CA 94708
(415) 841-8732 ▌P ♉ ⚓ GT ⑦

Directions	Located in Tilden Park, in Wildcat Canyon in the heart of the North Berkeley Hills, east of Berkeley; from Berkeley, take Spruce St. off University Ave. to Wildcat Canyon Rd.
Hours	Every day 10 A.M. to 5 P.M.; closed Christmas and New Year's days; guided tours, Saturday and Sunday, 2:30 P.M. without reservations; group tours available by advance reservation.
Admission	No fee.
Wheelchair access	Limited.
Special features	Children's petting zoo.

UNIVERSITY OF CALIFORNIA AT BERKELEY BOTANICAL GARDEN
Centennial Drive   Berkeley, CA 94720
(415) 642-3343 ▌P ♉ ⚓ GT ⑦ 🅼 ⚑

Directions	Located east of the Berkeley campus and Memorial Stadium; from San Francisco, take Rte. 580/80 (Eastshore Fwy.) north to University Ave. east; left on Oxford St.; right on Hearst St.; continue east to Centennial Dr., past stadium, to garden entrance.
Hours	9 A.M. to 4:45 P.M. every day except Christmas; guided tours, every Saturday and Sunday 1:30 P.M.; group tours by advance reservation.
Admission	No fee.
Wheelchair access	Most areas.
Special features	Horticultural library.

GREYSTONE PARK
905 Lomas Vista Drive   Beverly Hills, CA 90210
(213) 285-2537 **▤ P**

Directions	Located off Mulholland Dr. in Beverly Hills.
Hours	Every day 10 A.M. to 5 P.M.; closed holidays.
Admission	No fee.
Wheelchair access	Most areas.
Special features	Estate restoration.

VIRGINIA ROBINSON GARDENS
1008 Elden Way   Beverly Hills, CA 90210
(213) 276-4823 **▤ GT**

Directions	Provided at the time reservations are made.
Hours	Every day 9 A.M. to 5 P.M.; closed Christmas Day; because parking is extremely limited in the gardens' quiet residential area, advance reservations are required. Call the number above, or the County of Los Angeles Department of Arboreta and Botanic Gardens: (818) 446-8251.
Admission	Fee charged.
Wheelchair access	Limited.
Special features	Estate restoration.

RANCHO SANTA ANA BOTANIC GARDEN
1500 North College Avenue   Claremont, CA 91711-3101
(714) 625-8767 **▤ P ⏾ ⋔ GT ⑦ ⊠ ↵**

Directions	Located on College Avenue, north of Foothill Blvd. and east of Indian Hill Blvd., in Claremont; San Bernardino Fwy. (#10) to Indian Hill Blvd. exit; north 2 mi. to Foothill Blvd.; three blocks east to College Ave.; north on College into the garden visitor parking lot.
Hours	Every day 8 A.M. to 5 P.M.; closed July 4, Thanksgiving, Christmas, and New Year's days; guided tours, Sunday afternoon, March through May; group tours by advance reservation: (714) 626-1917; plant sale, first Saturday in November.
Admission	No fee.
Wheelchair access	Throughout.
Special features	Bookstore with wide selection of children's books on plants and animals.

SHERMAN LIBRARY AND GARDENS
2647 East Coast Highway   Corona del Mar, CA 92625
(714) 673-2261 ⬛P⌇✕🏛GT⑦Ⓜ↵

Directions	Located 40 mi. south of Los Angeles; Irvine Fwy. to Mac-Arthur Blvd. exit; south on MacArthur to Pacific Coast Hwy.; turn left and proceed 1 block to entrance.
Hours	Gardens, every day 10:30 A.M. to 4 P.M., except New Year's, Thanksgiving, and Christmas days; Historical Library, Monday through Friday 9 A.M. to 5 P.M.; Tea Garden (restaurant), November through April, Saturday through Monday, May through October, Saturday through Tuesday, 11 A.M. to 3 P.M.; group tours for 12 or more by advance (1 month) reservation.
Admission	Fee charged; no fee for children age 11 and under.
Wheelchair access	Throughout.
Special features	Historic restoration; Historical Library, with exhibits of interest to children as well as adults.

UNIVERSITY OF CALIFORNIA AT DAVIS ARBORETUM
University of California   Davis, CA 95616
(916) 752-2498 ⬛P⌇⚓GT Ⓜ↵

Directions	Davis is located about 90 mi. east of San Francisco and 15 mi. west of Sacramento; the arboretum is located just north of the I-80 exit, off California Ave.
Hours	Every day 24 hrs.; annual Plant Fair in early October; guided tours, 2 P.M. every Sunday.
Admission	No fee.
Wheelchair access	Throughout.
Special features	University campus.

QUAIL BOTANICAL GARDENS

P.O. Box 5   230 Quail Gardens Drive   Encinitas, CA 92024
(619) 434-3036 (Tuesday and Thursday 10 A.M. to 1 P.M.)
(619) 565-3600 (San Diego County Parks Department.) ⬛P♿⚲⚲GT⑦Ⓜ

Directions	Located 25 mi. north of San Diego; I-5 to Encinitas Blvd.; proceed east ½ mi., left (north) on Quail Gardens Dr.; ¼ mi. to gardens' entrance.
Hours	Gardens, every day 8 A.M. to 5 P.M., including holidays; gift shop and plant sales area, Wednesday, Friday, Saturday, and Sunday 11 A.M. to 3 P.M.; guided tours, every Saturday 10 A.M.; tours for children age 3 to 6, first Tuesday of every month 10:30 A.M.
Admission	No fee; fee charged for parking.
Wheelchair access	Throughout; wheelchairs available at the gift shop, Wednesday through Sunday 11 A.M. to 2:30 P.M.
Special features	Herbarium; library.

MENDOCINO COAST BOTANICAL GARDENS

18220 North Highway 1   Fort Bragg, CA 95437
(707) 964-4352 ⬛P♿⚲✗⚲

Directions	Located 1 mi. south of Fort Bragg and 6 mi. north of Mendocino on the Pacific Coast Hwy. (Rte. 1).
Hours	Every day 8 A.M. to dusk; closed holidays.
Admission	Fee charged; no fee for children age 12 and under.
Wheelchair access	Half the trails.
Special features	Retail nursery.

KRUSE RHODODENDRON STATE RESERVE

Fort Ross, CA

Mailing Address: Department of State Parks   25050 Coast Highway 1
Jenner, CA 94550
(707) 847-3221 ⬛P⚲

Directions	Located about 7 mi. north of the town of Fort Ross and about 100 mi. north of San Francisco, along the Pacific Coast Hwy.
Hours	Every day, dawn to dusk.
Admission	Fee charged.
Wheelchair access	None.
Special features	Camping facilities.

FULLERTON ARBORETUM
California State University Fullerton, CA 92634
(714) 773-3579 ▊P ᄆ ᎥᎥ GT ⑦ ▥ ◢

Directions	Fullerton is located about 25 mi. southeast of Los Angeles; the arboretum is situated in the northeast corner of the Cal. State campus, near the intersection of Yorba Linda Blvd. and Rte. 57.
Hours	Grounds, every day 8 A.M. to 4:45 P.M., except major holidays; Heritage House, Sunday 2 to 4 P.M., closed during August and major holidays; group tours by advance reservation; library, weekdays 8 A.M. to noon and 1 to 4 P.M. by appointment.
Admission	Grounds, no fee; Heritage House, fee charged.
Wheelchair access	Throughout.
Special features	Historic restoration; apiary; library; university campus.

UNIVERSITY OF CALIFORNIA AT IRVINE ARBORETUM
School of Biological Sciences Irvine, CA 92717
(714) 856-5833 ▊P ᄆ ⚐ GT ▥

Directions	Located on the UCI campus, off Campus Dr.; I-405 to the Jamboree exit; left on Campus Dr.
Hours	Monday through Friday 8:30 A.M. to 3:30 P.M.; closed Saturday, Sunday and all federal holidays.
Admission	No fee.
Wheelchair access	Limited.
Special features	University campus.

DESCANSO GARDENS
1418 Descanso Drive La Cañada Flintridge, CA 91011
(818) 790-5571 ▊P ᄆ ✕ ᎥᎥ GT ⑦ ▥ ◢

Directions	Located within easy driving distance of Los Angeles, Glendale, Pasadena, and the San Fernando Valley; take Fwy. 210 or Foothill Blvd. to Descanso Drive.
Hours	Every day 9 A.M. to 5 P.M., closed Christmas Day; Cafe Court, every day 10 A.M. to 3 P.M.; Japanese Tea House, every day 11 A.M. to 4 P.M., closed Monday.
Admission	Fee charged; free admission on the third Tuesday of every month.
Wheelchair access	Throughout.
Special features	Art gallery.

THE HORTENSE MILLER GARDEN
P.O. Box 742 Laguna Beach, CA 92652
(714) 497-0716 ◧ **P** ⛾ **GT** 🏛

Directions	Laguna Beach is located along the Pacific coast, about 50 mi. south of Los Angeles; the garden is located just off the Pacific Coast Hwy.
Hours	Tuesday through Friday and Saturday morning; closed national holidays; natural history and horticultural library open one day each month; all visits are by guided tour arranged in advance with Laguna Beach City Hall; write for an appointment, or call during business hours (see above tel. no.); complete tour takes from 2 to 3 hrs.
Admission	No fee.
Wheelchair access	Throughout.
Special features	Estate restoration.

RANCHO LOS ALAMITOS HISTORIC SITE AND GARDENS
6400 Bixby Hill Road Long Beach, CA 90815
(213) 431-3541 ◧ **P** 🏚 **GT**

Directions	Long Beach is situated on the coast, about 20 mi. south of Los Angeles; the ranch is located near Cal. State Long Beach and the intersection of the Pacific Coast Hwy. and 7th St.
Hours	Wednesday through Sunday 1 to 5 P.M.; tours every half hour, with the last at 4 P.M.; group tours by advance reservation.
Admission	No fee.
Wheelchair access	Main house, some of the gardens, and all but two of the barns.
Special features	Historic restoration; working blacksmith shop.

MILDRED E. MATHIAS BOTANICAL GARDEN
University of California 405 Hilgard Avenue Los Angeles, CA 90024-1606
(213) 825-3620 ◧ **P** ⛾ ⚐ **GT**

Directions	Located in the southeastern part of the UCLA campus; entrances are at intersection of Le Conte and Hilgard Aves. and at north end of the garden, below the Botany Bldg. (Tiverton Dr. and Circle Dr. South).
Hours	8 A.M. to 5 P.M. Monday through Friday, 8 A.M. to 4 P.M. Saturday and Sunday; closed on university holidays.
Admission	No fee; fee charged for campus parking facility.
Wheelchair access	Most areas.
Special features	University campus.

UCLA HANNAH CARTER JAPANESE GARDEN
University of California   10619 Bellagio Road   Los Angeles, CA 90024-1606
(213) 825-3620 ∎ P ⚲ **GT**

Directions	From Sunset Blvd. turn north onto Stone Canyon Rd.; proceed to stop sign; bear left onto Bellagio Rd. and continue to no. 10619, just beyond the first two homes at the intersection of Stone Canyon and Bellagio Rds.
Hours	Open by reservation only: Tuesday 10 A.M. to 1 P.M., Wednesday noon to 3 P.M.; phone UCLA Visitor Center: (213) 825-4574.
Admission	No fee.
Wheelchair access	None.

THE J. PAUL GETTY MUSEUM
17985 Pacific Coast Highway   Malibu, CA 90265-5799

Mailing Address: P.O. Box 2112   Santa Monica, CA 90406
(213) 458-2003 ∎ P ✗ ⅲ **GT** ⊘

Directions	Located on the Pacific Coast Hwy. between Sunset and Topanga Canyon Blvds., approximately 25 mi. west of downtown Los Angeles.
Hours	Tuesday through Sunday 10 A.M. to 5 P.M.; closed New Year's, Independence, Thanksgiving, and Christmas days.
Admission	No fee; it is advisable to call in advance of visit for parking reservations: (213) 458-2003, 9 A.M. to 5 P.M., seven days a week.
Wheelchair access	Throughout.
Special features	Museum of historic art and artifacts.

MUIR WOODS NATIONAL MONUMENT
United States Department of the Interior   National Park Service
Mill Valley, CA 94941
(415) 388-2595 ∎ P ✗ ⅲ ⊘

Directions	Located 17 mi. north of San Francisco; take U.S. Rte. 101 or State Rte. 1; follow signs.
Hours	Every day 8 A.M. to dusk; advisable to visit during morning hours to avoid midday crowds.
Admission	No fee.
Wheelchair access	Limited to paved trails, which are extensive.

DUNSMUIR HOUSE AND GARDENS
2960 Peralta Oaks Court   Oakland, CA 94605
(415) 562-0328 **P ⚓ GT** Ⓜ

Directions	From Oakland, take Rte. 580 east to the 106th Ave. exit; go left under the fwy.; follow signs to Dunsmuir.
Hours	Sundays noon to 4 P.M., April through September; guided tours, Sunday and Wednesday at 11:30 A.M., 12:30 and 1:30 P.M.; group tours by advance reservation.
Admission	Grounds, no fee; fee charged for house tour.
Wheelchair access	Throughout.
Special features	Estate restoration; children's playhouse.

LAKESIDE PARK GARDEN CENTER
666 Bellevue Avenue   Oakland, CA 94612
(415) 273-2199

Mailing address: Lakeside Park Garden Center   Oakland Office of Parks and Recreation   1520 Lakeside Drive   Oakland, CA 94612
(415) 273-3090 **P ⚐ ⚓ ✕ ⅲ GT** ⓘ

Directions	Located within Lakeside Park, along its main roadway (Bellevue Ave.) which forks to the south off Oakland's Grand Ave.
Hours	Garden Center, Monday through Friday 10 A.M. to 3 P.M., weekends 10 A.M. to 4 P.M.; park, every day, dawn to dusk.; guided group tours by advance reservation.
Admission	No fee.
Wheelchair access	Limited.
Special features	Natural science center; amusement park for children.

THE OAKLAND MUSEUM AND GARDENS
1000 Oak Street   Oakland, CA 94607
(415) 273-3401 **P ✕ ⅲ GT** Ⓜ

Directions	Located adjacent to Lake Merritt and four blocks east of Hwy. 880 (Nimitz Fwy.).
Hours	Wednesday through Saturday 10 A.M. to 5 P.M., Sunday noon to 7 P.M.; tours, Wednesday, Thursday, and Friday at 2 P.M.; group tours by 1-month advance reservation; closed Monday, Tuesday, July 4, Thanksgiving, Christmas, and New Year's days.
Admission	No fee; fee charged for parking.
Wheelchair access	Throughout.
Special features	Art, culture, and natural history exhibits.

THE LIVING DESERT
47-900 Portola Avenue   Palm Desert, CA 92260
(619) 346-5694 ∎ P ⬚ ⬚ ⬚ ✕ ⬚ GT ⬚

Directions	Located 150 mi. from Los Angeles; east on I-10 to Bob Hope Dr. exit; south to Hwy. 111 to Portola Ave.; south 1½ mi.
Hours	Every day 9 A.M. to 5 P.M.; closed June 16 to August 31; group tours of 15 or more by advance reservation.
Admission	Fee charged; no fee for children age 5 and under.
Wheelchair access	Throughout.
Special features	Animal shows; concerts and lectures; native plant shop.

MOORTEN BOTANICAL GARDEN
1701 South Palm Canyon Drive   Palm Springs, CA 92264
(619) 327-6555 ∎ P ⬚ GT

Directions	Located at the south end of Palm Springs, at the point where South Palm Canyon Dr. makes a 90-degree turn to become East Palm Canyon Dr.
Hours	Every day 9 A.M. to 5 P.M.; group tours by advance reservation.
Admission	Fee charged.
Wheelchair access	Throughout.
Special features	Estate restoration; pioneer and Native-American artifacts.

ELIZABETH F. GAMBLE GARDEN CENTER
1431 Waverly Street   Palo Alto, CA 94301
(415) 329-1356 ∎ P ⬚ GT ⬚ ⬚ ⬚

Directions	El Camino Real or U.S. 1 to Embarcadero Rd.; proceed to stoplight at Waverly St.; garden is located on southeast corner, with entrance on Waverly St.
Hours	Gardens, every day, dawn to dusk; visitor center (office), Monday through Friday 9 A.M. to noon; library, Monday through Thursday noon to 3 P.M.; guided tours by advance reservation; Master Gardener's Hotline in operation every Friday 1 to 4 P.M.
Admission	No fee.
Wheelchair access	Throughout.
Special features	Estate restoration.

SOUTH COAST BOTANIC GARDEN
26300 Crenshaw Boulevard   Palos Verdes Peninsula, CA 90274
(213) 377-0468 ∎P♓🏛GT⑦Ⓜ↲

Directions	Located about 20 mi. south of downtown Los Angeles;· San Diego Fwy. (I-405) to Crenshaw Blvd. south to the garden.
Hours	Every day 9 A.M. to 5 P.M.; closed Christmas Day.
Admission	Fee charged; no fee for children age 4 and under; fee for tram tour.
Wheelchair access	Throughout.

THE EDDY ARBORETUM
Institute of Forest Genetics   2480 Carson Road   Placerville, CA 95667
(916) 622-1225 ∎P♓⑦

Directions	Located approximately 40 mi. east of Sacramento and 3 mi. outside of Placerville; take U.S. 50 east through Placerville; left on Carson Rd.; continue past intersection of Union Ridge Rd.; institute entrance is on the right.
Hours	Monday through Friday 8 A.M. to 4:30 P.M.; group tours by advance reservation.
Admission	No fee.
Wheelchair access	Limited.
Special features	Research and breeding facility.

UNIVERSITY OF CALIFORNIA AT RIVERSIDE BOTANIC GARDENS
Riverside, CA 92521
(714) 787-4650 ∎P♓GT⑦Ⓜ

Directions	Riverside is located 56 mi. east of Los Angeles' city center; I-215/State Hwy. 60 to University Ave. exit; follow signs to campus entrance; once inside campus, follow Campus Dr. to Parking Lot 13; enter Lot 13 to reach the cedar-lined drive to the botanic gardens entrance and free parking area.
Hours	Every day 8 A.M. to 5 P.M.; closed New Year's, Independence, Thanksgiving, and Christmas days; guided tours by advance reservation.
Admission	No fee; contributions accepted.
Wheelchair access	Most areas.
Special features	University campus.

MARIN ART AND GARDEN CENTER
P.O. Box 437   Sir Francis Drake Boulevard   Ross, CA 94957-0437
(415) 454-5597 ▪ P ✕ ⅲ GT ▣

Directions	Located at the intersection of Sir Francis Drake Blvd. and Laurel Grove Ave.
Hours	Every day 9 A.M. to 4 P.M.; guided tours by advance (at least 2 weeks) reservation.
Admission	No fee.
Wheelchair access	Throughout.
Special features	Historic restoration; library; theater; art gallery.

BALBOA PARK
Park & Recreation Department   Balboa Park Maintenance Center
San Diego, CA 92101
(619) 236-5984 ▪ P ⊥ ✕ ⅲ ⓘ

Directions	Located in downtown San Diego, just east of Rte. 163.
Hours	Grounds, every day, dawn to dusk; Botanical Building, every day 10 A.M. to 4 P.M., closed Wednesday and holidays.
Admission	No fee.
Wheelchair access	Most areas.
Special features	Indoor and outdoor theaters; museums; zoo; recreational facilities.

THE SAN DIEGO ZOO
The Zoological Society of San Diego   P.O. Box 551   San Diego, CA 92112-0551
Zoo: (619) 234-3153 or (619) 231-1515
Wild Animal Park: (619) 234-6541 or (619) 480-0100 ▪ P ✕ ⅲ ▣

Directions	Zoo is located in downtown San Diego in the northwest corner of Balboa Park; I-5 to Park Boulevard exit north; Wild Animal Park is located east of Escondido; I-15 north to Via Rancho Pkwy.; follow signs to the park on Hwy. 78 (San Pasqual Valley Rd.).
Hours	Every day, Labor Day through June, 9 A.M. to 4 P.M.; July through Labor Day, 9 A.M. to 5 P.M.
Admission	Fee charged; no fee for children age 2 and under.
Wheelchair access	Most areas; wheelchairs and strollers may be rented.
Special features	Children's zoo.

CONSERVATORY OF FLOWERS
Recreation and Parks Department   Golden Gate Park   Fell and Stanyan Streets
San Francisco, CA 94117
(415) 666-7106 ▊Ⴓ⚓

Directions	Conservatory located at the eastern end of Golden Gate Park, which is situated in western San Francisco, bordered by Fulton and Stanyan Sts. and Lincoln Way.
Hours	Conservatory, every day; in winter 9 A.M. to 5 P.M., summer 9 A.M. to 6 P.M.; nearby Japanese tea garden, every day 8 A.M. to 5:30 P.M.
Admission	Conservatory, fee charged every day except national holidays; Japanese tea garden, fee charged every day except first Wednesday of every month and national holidays; no fee for children age 5 and under at either conservatory or Japanese tea garden.
Wheelchair access	Throughout.
Special features	Located within Golden Gate Park are a museum, a planetarium, and an aquarium, in addition to all kinds of recreational facilities.

STRYBING ARBORETUM AND BOTANICAL GARDENS
Ninth Avenue at Lincoln Way   San Francisco, CA 94122

Mailing address: Strybing Arboretum Society   Ninth Avenue at Martin Luther King Drive   San Francisco, CA 94122
(415) 661-1316 ▊Ⴓ⚓ⅲ**GT**⊘▨⤴

Directions	Golden Gate Park is located at the western end of San Francisco, bordered by Lincoln Way and Fulton and Stanyan Sts.; Fell St. west leads to the park from downtown San Francisco; arboretum is located at Ninth Ave. and Lincoln Way.
Hours	Arboretum, weekdays 8 A.M. to 4:30 P.M.; weekends and holidays 10 A.M. to 5 P.M.; library, every day 10 A.M. to 4 P.M., closed major holidays; guided tours, weekdays 1:30 P.M., weekends 10:30 A.M. and 1:30 P.M.
Admission	No fee.
Wheelchair access	Throughout.
Special features	Reference library with rare books and art exhibits; bookstore; twice monthly plant sale.

OVERFELT GARDENS

San Jose Department of Recreation, Parks & Community Services
333 West Santa Clara Street, Suite 800   San Jose, CA 95113
(408) 251-3323 or (408) 926-5555 ∎ P ⚖ GT

Directions	Located at the intersection of McKee Rd. and Educational Park Dr.; parking lot is adjacent to the San Jose Public Library.
Hours	Every day 10 A.M. to dusk; Park Rangers available for group tours; call either of the above numbers for information.
Admission	No fee.
Wheelchair access	Throughout.
Special features	Chinese pavilions and structures.

HUNTINGTON BOTANICAL GARDENS

1151 Oxford Road   San Marino, CA 91108
(818) 405-2100 ∎ P ⚱ ✕ 𝓲 GT

Directions	Located 12 mi. northeast of downtown Los Angeles; Pasadena Fwy. (Rte. 110) north to California Blvd.; west to Oxford Rd.
Hours	Tuesday through Sunday 1 to 4:30 P.M.; closed during October; guided tours, Tuesday through Saturday 1 P.M.; group tours by advance reservation; Patio Restaurant, 1 to 4 P.M.; gift shop, 12:30 to 5 P.M.
Admission	No fee (donation of $2 suggested).
Wheelchair access	Throughout.
Special features	Library; art galleries.

SAN MATEO JAPANESE GARDEN
Department of Parks and Recreation   330 West 20th Avenue
San Mateo, CA 94403-1388
(415) 377-4700

SAN MATEO ARBORETUM
San Mateo Arboretum Society   P.O. Box 1523   San Mateo, CA 64401 **∎P⊥⋏⋏**

Directions	Japanese garden is located at the intersection of Laurel and Fifth Aves. in Central Park in downtown San Mateo.
Hours	Japanese garden, Monday through Friday 9 A.M. to 4 P.M.; Saturday, Sunday, and holidays 11 A.M. to 5 P.M.; arboretum, every day, dawn to dusk.
Admission	No fee for either the park or Japanese garden.
Wheelchair access	Throughout.
Special features	Children's train; recreational facilities.

HEARST SAN SIMEON STATE HISTORICAL MONUMENT
Department of Parks and Recreation   P.O. Box 8   Highway 1
San Simeon, CA 93452-0040
(805) 927-2020 **∎P⊥⋏GT②**

Directions	Located just off California Hwy. 1, east of San Simeon Village; the entrance is well marked.
Hours	Every day except Thanksgiving, Christmas, and New Year's days; tours start at 8:20 A.M., and the last begins at 3 P.M. in winter, later in summer; advance reservations are advisable; call (800) 444-7275.
Admission	Fee charged.
Wheelchair access	Special tour arrangements must be made at least 10 days before scheduled visit: (805) 927-3624.
Special features	Estate restoration.

SANTA BARBARA BOTANIC GARDEN
1212 Mission Canyon Road   Santa Barbara, CA 93105
(805) 682-4726 ▐ P ▽ ⅲ GT ⑦ Ⓜ ↵

Directions	Located north of downtown Santa Barbara; Hwy. 192 (Foothill Rd.) to Mission Canyon Rd.; north on Mission Canyon Rd. to garden entrance on the left.
Hours	Grounds, every day 8 A.M. to dusk; gift shop, every day except Christmas 10 A.M. to 4 P.M.; nursery, Tuesday, Thursday, Friday, and Saturday 10 A.M. to 3 P.M., Sunday 11 A.M. to 3 P.M.; guided tours, Sunday and Thursday 10:30 A.M.; library and herbarium by appointment only.
Admission	Fee charged every day except Tuesdays and Wednesdays; no fee any time for children age 4 and under.
Wheelchair access	Limited.
Special features	Herbarium; horticultural library; plant nursery.

UNIVERSITY OF CALIFORNIA AT SANTA CRUZ ARBORETUM
Santa Cruz, CA 95064
(408) 427-2998 ▐ P ▽ ⅲ GT ↵

Directions	Santa Cruz is located on the Pacific coast, about 70 mi. south of San Francisco; the arboretum is located on the UC campus; entrance is off Empire Grade, about ¼ mi. northwest of the intersection of Empire Grade and Western Dr.
Hours	Every day 9 A.M. to 5 P.M.; guided tours, Wednesday, Saturday, and Sunday 2 to 4 P.M.
Admission	No fee.
Wheelchair access	Most areas.
Special features	University campus.

HAKONE GARDENS
City of Saratoga   13777 Fruitvale Avenue   Saratoga, CA 95070
(408) 867-3438 ❚P⌁👥GT ⑦ Ⓜ

Directions	Saratoga is located about 40 mi. south of San Francisco; the gardens are situated at 21000 Big Basin Way.
Hours	Weekdays 10 A.M. to 5 P.M., weekends 11 A.M. to 5 P.M., closed legal holidays; guided tours and tea service, Saturday and Sunday 1 to 4 P.M., April through September; group tours by advance reservation.
Admission	No fee; donations accepted.
Wheelchair access	Most areas.
Special features	Estate restoration.

VILLA MONTALVO ARBORETUM
15400 Montalvo Road   P.O. Box 158   Saratoga, CA 95071-0158
(408) 741-3421 ❚P☕👥GT ⑦

Directions	Located about 50 mi. south of San Francisco and 15 mi. west of San Jose, along the Saratoga-Los Gatos Rd.
Hours	Arboretum, weekdays 8 A.M. to 5 P.M., weekends 9 A.M. to 5 P.M.; gallery, Friday 1 to 4 P.M., weekends 11 A.M. to 4 P.M.; tours of mansion and carriage house scheduled regularly; grounds are closed during certain special events; call ahead to be sure the arboretum is open.
Admission	Grounds, no fee; fee status is being reconsidered; call to determine whether or not an admission fee is required.
Wheelchair access	Most areas.
Special features	Estate restoration; bird sanctuary; art gallery.

PAGEANT OF ROSES GARDEN
Rose Hills Memorial Park   3900 South Workman Mill Road   P.O. Box 110
Whittier, CA 90608
(213) 699-0921 ❚P☕👥 ⑦

Directions	Whittier is located about 12 mi. east of Los Angeles' city center; take Fwy. 605 to the Rose Hills Rd. exit; Rose Hills Rd. to Workman Mill Rd.; turn left and continue to Park entrance on the right; the Rose Garden is just inside the entrance.
Hours	Spring and summer months, every day 8 A.M. to dusk.
Admission	No fee.
Wheelchair access	Throughout.
Special features	Children's art festival.

FILOLI
Cañada Road   Woodside, CA 94062
(415) 364-2880 ▪P✕ⅲGT Ⓜ

Directions	Woodside is located approximately 25 mi. from San Francisco and 12 mi. from the San Francisco Airport; from San Francisco, take I-280 south; west on Edgewood Rd.; north on Cañada Rd.; entrance is about 1 mi. up on the left.
Hours	Mid-February to mid-November, Tuesday through Saturday; all visits are by reservation made well in advance for group tours of the house and gardens (lasting about 2 hrs.); call the above number Monday through Friday, 9 A.M. to 3 P.M.; guided nature hikes of the undeveloped portions, covering the Ohlone Indian dig, wildlife areas, and the San Andreas fault, available weekdays and Saturday morning, also by advance reservation.
Admission	Fee charged.
Wheelchair access	Limited; notify in advance so that special arrangements can be made.
Special features	Estate restoration.

HAWAII

LILIUOKALANI GARDENS

Department of Parks and Recreation   25 Aupuni Street, Room 210
Hilo, Hawaii, HI 96720
(808) 961-8311 **P⚓**

Directions	Located in Hilo, at the intersection of Rtes. 200 and 11, on the island of Hawaii.
Hours	Every day, dawn to dusk.
Admission	No fee.
Wheelchair access	Limited.

NANI MAU GARDENS

421 Makalika Street   Hilo, Hawaii, HI 96720
(808) 959-3541 **◼ P ☖ ✗ 🏛 GT ⑦**

Directions	Located 3 mi. south of downtown Hilo, off Hwy. 11 on the way to Hawaii Volcanoes National Park; watch for the Hawaii Visitors Bureau warrior marker that indicates the turnoff onto Makalika St.
Hours	Every day 8 A.M. to 5 P.M.
Admission	Fee charged.
Wheelchair access	Limited; narrated tram tours and golf carts available.

OLA PUA BOTANICAL GARDEN AND PLANTATION

Box 518   Kalaheo, Kauai, HI 96741
(808) 332-8182 **◼ P ☖ ⚓ GT**

Directions	Located on Hwy. 50, just past the city of Kalaheo, in the direction of Waimea Canyon.
Hours	All visits by guided tours only, Monday through Friday 9:30 and 11:30 A.M. and 1:30 P.M.
Admission	Fee charged.
Wheelchair access	Most areas.
Special features	Estate restoration.

MOIR'S GARDENS
Rural Route 1 P.O. Box 73   Koloa, Kauai, HI 96756
(808) 742-6411 **P ✕ ⅲ**

Directions	Located on Kauai's south shore, along Poipu Beach.
Hours	Every day 8:30 A.M. to 4:30 P.M.
Admission	No fee.
Wheelchair access	Limited.
Special features	Beachside resort hotel.

NATIONAL TROPICAL BOTANICAL GARDEN
P.O. Box 340   Lawai, Kauai, HI 96765
(808) 332-7361 **⬛ P ⛾ ⅲ GT ⑦ ▥**

Directions	Located on the southern coast of the island of Kauai; Rte. 50 to the Lawai turnoff (Rte. 530); right on Hailima Rd.
Hours	Tours of the garden, including the Allerton Estate, lasting 2½ to 3 hrs., by advance reservation only; call the above number Monday through Sunday 7:30 A.M. to 4 P.M.; museum and gift shop open Monday through Friday 7:45 A.M. to 4 P.M.
Admission	Fee charged for tours.
Wheelchair access	Museum and gift shop only.
Special features	Botanical museum.

KAHANU GARDENS
P.O. Box 45   Hana, Maui, HI 96713
(808) 248-8912 **⬛ P ⅲ ▥**

Directions	Follow the Hana Hwy. to Ulaino Rd., just past mile marker no. 31; left on Ulaino Rd. and continue for about 1½ mi.; garden entrance is on the left.
Hours	Tuesday through Saturday 10 A.M. to 2 P.M.; group tours by advance reservation.
Admission	Fee charged; no fee for children age 11 and under.
Wheelchair access	Throughout.
Special features	Ancient Polynesian temple.

KULA BOTANICAL GARDENS
RR 2 Box 288 Kula, Maui, HI 96790
(808) 878-1715 ▊ P ⛾ ✗ ⚏ GT

Directions	Located about a mile from Kula Hwy. on Kekaulike Rd.
Hours	Every day 9 A.M. to 4 P.M.; guided tours for groups by two-week advance reservation.
Admission	Fee charged; no fee for children age 5 and under.
Wheelchair access	Throughout.

WAIMEA FALLS PARK ARBORETUM AND BOTANICAL GARDENS
59-864 Kamehameha Highway Haleiwa, Oahu, HI 96712
(808) 638-8511 ▊ P ⛾ ✗ ⚏ GT ⑦

Directions	Haleiwa is located about 40 mi. from Honolulu's city center, on the north shore of Oahu; the arboretum and botanical gardens are located about 3 mi. north of Haleiwa.
Hours	Every day 10 A.M. to 5:30 P.M.
Admission	Fee charged; no fee for children age 3 and under.
Wheelchair access	Throughout.
Special features	Hula dancing and cliff-diving performances.

FOSTER BOTANIC GARDEN
50 North Vineyard Boulevard Honolulu, Oahu, HI 96817
(808) 533-3406 ▊ P ⛾ ✗ ⚏ GT ⑦ ▣ ♫

Directions	Located on the island of Oahu in downtown Honolulu, at the intersection of North Vineyard Blvd. and Nuuanu Ave.
Hours	Every day 9 A.M. to 4 P.M., except Christmas and New Year's days.
Admission	Fee charged; no fee for children age 11 and under.
Wheelchair access	Throughout.

HAROLD L. LYON ARBORETUM
University of Hawaii at Manoa   3860 Manoa Road   Honolulu, Oahu, HI 96822
(808) 988-3177 ∎ P ⛲ ⛶ GT ⌂ ♪

Directions	Located north of downtown Honolulu, near Paradise Park in the upper Manoa Valley; take Punahou St. north; bear left at the fork, and continue north on Manoa Rd.
Hours	Monday through Friday 9 A.M. to 3 P.M.; Saturday 9 A.M. to noon; guided tours on first Friday and third Wednesday of every month at 1 P.M., and third Saturday at 10 A.M.; group tours by advance reservation.
Admission	No fee; small donation suggested.
Wheelchair access	None.

MOANALUA GARDENS
1352 Pineapple Place   Honolulu, Oahu, HI 96819
(808) 839-5334 ∎ P ⛲ GT ⑦

Directions	Located off Puuloa Rd. and Mahiale St. in greater Honolulu.
Hours	Every day 7 A.M. to 6:30 P.M. in summer, 7 A.M. to 6 P.M. in winter; group tours by advance reservation.
Admission	No fee; donations requested for guided tours.
Wheelchair access	Limited.
Special features	Historic restoration.

QUEEN EMMA SUMMER PALACE
2913 Pali Highway   Honolulu, Oahu, HI 96817
(808) 595-6291 ∎ P ⛶

Directions	Located a few miles from Honolulu's city center on the Pali Hwy.
Hours	Every day 9 A.M. to 4 P.M.
Admission	No fee.
Wheelchair access	Throughout.
Special features	Historic restoration; museum.

HO'OMALUHIA
Honolulu Botanic Gardens P.O. Box 1116 Kane'ohe, Oahu, HI 96744
(808) 235-6636 ∎ P ⊊ ⚓ **GT** ⊘ ⤺

Directions	Kane'ohe is located on the east coast of Oahu, about 16 mi. from Honolulu's city center; from Honolulu, take Pali Hwy. north; west on Kamehameha Hwy.; left on Luluku Rd. and continue to the park entrance.
Hours	Every day 9 A.M. to 4 P.M., closed Christmas and New Year's days; guided nature hikes, every Saturday at 10 A.M. and every Sunday at 1 P.M.; camping by permit only; call above number for information.
Admission	No fee.
Wheelchair access	Most areas.
Special features	Camping facilities; horseback-riding trails.

WAHIAWA BOTANIC GARDEN
1396 California Avenue Wahiawa, Oahu, HI 96786
(808) 621-7321 ∎ P ⊊ **GT** ⊘

Directions	The city of Wahiawa is located about 18 mi. northwest of Honolulu's city center, in central Oahu, midway between the Waianae Mountains and the Koolau Range; the garden is located at 1396 California Ave.
Hours	Every day 9 A.M. to 4 P.M., except Christmas and New Year's days; guided tours by advance reservation.
Admission	No fee.
Wheelchair access	Throughout.

OREGON

JENKINS ESTATE
Tualatin Hills Park & Recreation District P.O. Box 5868 Aloha, OR 97006
(503) 642-3855 **P ⍦ ⚓ GT**

Directions	Located 16 mi. west of Portland, at S.W. 209th and Farmington Rd., off Grabhorn Rd.
Hours	Garden, Monday through Friday 8 A.M. to 4 P.M.; end of May to end of September, Monday through Thursday 8 A.M. to 8 P.M., Friday 8 A.M. to 4 P.M.; house, Monday through Friday by appointment only; guided tours of house and gardens by advance reservation.
Admission	No fee.
Wheelchair access	Limited.
Special features	Estate restoration.

SHORE ACRES STATE PARK GARDEN
13030 Cape Arago Highway P.O. Box 1172 Coos Bay, OR 97420
(503) 888-3732 **P ⍦ ⚓ ⋔ GT ⊘**

Directions	Located about 12 mi. southwest of Coos Bay.
Hours	Every day, 8 A.M. to dusk.
Admission	No fee; fee charged for parking, Memorial Day to Labor Day.
Wheelchair access	Throughout.
Special features	Estate grounds restoration.

GREER GARDENS
1280 Goodpasture Island Road Eugene, OR 97401
(503) 686-8266 **P ⍦ ⋔ GT**

Directions	From Portland, I-5 to Beltline Rd. west to Delta Hwy. south to Goodpasture Island Rd. east.
Hours	Monday through Saturday 8:30 A.M. to 5:30 P.M., Sunday 11 A.M. to 5 P.M.
Admission	No fee.
Wheelchair access	Limited.
Special features	Commercial nursery.

HENDRICK'S PARK RHODODENDRON GARDEN
Parks Services Division   210 Cheshire Street   Eugene, OR 97401
(503) 687-5333 or (503) 687-5334 **P .₄ GT**

Directions	Located along Summit Ave.; from Franklin Blvd. (Hwy. 99), turn south onto Walnut St.; turn east onto Summit Ave.
Hours	Every day, dawn to dusk; group tours by advance reservation.
Admission	No fee.
Wheelchair access	Throughout.
Special features	Children's play area.

THE MOUNT PISGAH ARBORETUM
P.O. Box 5621   Eugene, OR 97405
(503) 747-3817 **P ⫞ .₄ GT ⦵ ▥ ⌗**

Directions	Located along the Willamette River, within the Howard Buford Recreation Area in Lane County, southeast of Eugene and south of Springfield.
Hours	Every day, dawn to dusk.
Admission	No fee.
Wheelchair access	Limited.
Special features	Children's self-guiding nature trail.

OWEN ROSE GARDEN
Parks Services Division   210 Cheshire Street   Eugene, OR 97401
(503) 687-5333 or (503) 687-5334 **P ⫞ .₄**

Directions	Located off 1st Ave., on the south bank of the Willamette River; take Washington St. north; left on 1st Ave.; right on Jefferson St.
Hours	Every day, dawn to dusk.
Admission	No fee.
Wheelchair access	Throughout.

JOHN INSKEEP ENVIRONMENTAL LEARNING CENTER
19600 South Molalla Avenue   Oregon City, OR 97236
(503) 657-6958, ext. 351 ∎**P GT** ⑦

Directions	Oregon City is located southeast of Portland, near the intersection of Rte. 99E and I-205.
Hours	Garden, every day 9 A.M. to dusk; office, Tuesday through Friday 9 A.M. to 5 P.M.
Admission	No fee.
Wheelchair access	Throughout.
Special features	Wildlife exhibits; astronomical observatory; call for night-viewing schedules.

THE BERRY BOTANIC GARDEN
11505 S.W. Summerville Avenue   Portland, OR 97219
(503) 636-4112   ∎ ♉ **GT** 🖾

Directions	Located in a residential area between Lake Oswego and the city of Portland.
Hours	9 A.M. to 4 P.M. Monday through Saturday. Due to limited parking, all visits are by appointment only; call (503) 636-4112 on Tuesday or Thursday between 9 A.M. and 5 P.M.
Admission	No fee.
Wheelchair access	Limited.

CRYSTAL SPRINGS RHODODENDRON GARDEN
SE 28th Avenue at Woodstock Boulevard   Portland, OR 97202

Mailing address: Portland Park Bureau   1120 SW Fifth Avenue
Portland, OR 97204
(503) 771-8386 or 796-5193 ∎**P GT** ↩

Directions	Located in southeast Portland, adjacent to the Eastmoreland Golf Course and Reed College.
Hours	Every day, dawn to dusk.
Admission	No fee.
Wheelchair access	Throughout.

THE GROTTO

P.O. Box 20008   Portland, OR 97220
(503) 254-7371   ▌P ⚲ 📷 **GT** ⊘

Directions	Located just off I-205, at the intersection of Sandy Blvd. and N.E. 85th Ave., 20 mins. from downtown Portland and 10 mins. from Portland International Airport.
Hours	May through September, every day 9 A.M. to 6 P.M.; October through April, weekdays 10 A.M. to 4:30 P.M., weekends 9 A.M. to 5 P.M.; group tours by advance reservation.
Admission	No fee; fee charged for special events and festivals; small fee for use of the elevator.
Wheelchair access	Throughout.
Special features	Shrines; chapels; monastery.

HOYT ARBORETUM

4000 Fairview Boulevard   Portland, OR 97221
(503) 228-8732   ▌P ⚲ **GT** ⊘ ↵

Directions	From downtown Portland, Hwy. 26W to the Zoo-OMSI exit; follow main road through zoo parking lot; turn right on Fairview Blvd.
Hours	Garden, every day 6 A.M. to midnight; visitor center, 10 A.M. to 4 P.M.
Admission	No fee.
Wheelchair access	Throughout.

INTERNATIONAL ROSE TEST GARDEN AT WASHINGTON PARK
400 S.W. Kingston Boulevard   Portland, OR 97201
(503) 248-4302

Mailing address: City of Portland   Bureau of Parks and Public Recreation
6437 S.E. Division Street   Portland, OR 97206   **⌷P ⌷.⊥✕ GT**

Directions	Located in Washington Park in downtown Portland; follow signs in the park to the garden.
Hours	Every day 6 A.M. to 9 P.M.
Admission	No fee.
Wheelchair access	Throughout the garden.
Special features	Nearby Shakespeare garden.

THE JAPANESE GARDEN AT WASHINGTON PARK
Kingston Boulevard   Portland, OR 97201
(503) 223-1321

Mailing address: The Japanese Garden Society of Oregon   P.O. Box 3847
Portland, OR 97208   **⌷P GT**

Directions	Located in Washington Park, off Kingston Blvd., above the International Rose Test Garden; signs direct the way to the garden.
Hours	April 1 to September 30, every day 10 A.M. to 6 P.M.; October 1 to March 31, every day 10 A.M. to 4 P.M.; closed Thanksgiving, Christmas, and New Year's days.
Admission	Fee charged.
Wheelchair access	Limited.

LEACH BOTANICAL GARDEN
6704 S.E. 122nd Avenue   Portland, OR 97236
(503) 761-9503   **⌷P ⌷ ⋔ GT ⑦ ▥**

Directions	Located 20 mins. southeast of downtown Portland; follow either Powell Blvd. or I-205 to Foster Rd.; continue south on Foster Rd.; turn right at 122nd Ave. and continue for about ⅛ mile to garden entrance at Johnson Creek.
Hours	Tuesday to Saturday 10 A.M. to 4 P.M. all year; Sunday 10 A.M. to 4 P.M., February to December 10, 1 to 4 P.M., December to February; closed Monday, Thanksgiving, Christmas, and New Year's days, and July 4.
Admission	No fee.
Wheelchair access	Manor house and surrounding patios only; trails are steep and rugged.
Special features	Manor house with library.

THE BLOEDEL RESERVE
7571 N.E. Dolphin Drive   Bainbridge Island, WA 98110-1097
(206) 842-7631 ▊P⚌ GT ⊘

Directions	Bainbridge Island is reached via the Seattle-Winslow ferry from Seattle, or the Agate Pass Bridge from the Olympic Peninsula; both cases, take Rte. 305, turn north onto Dolphin Dr. and continue to the Reserve.
Hours	Wednesday through Sunday, except federal holidays, 10 A.M. to 4 P.M.; all visits by advance reservation only; call the above number.
Admission	Fee charged; no fee for children age 5 and under.
Wheelchair access	Most areas.
Special features	Estate restoration.

THE HERBFARM
32804 Issaquah-Fall City Road   Fall City, WA 98024
(206) 784-2222 ▊P ⚏✗⋔ GT ⬱

Directions	Located about 30 mins. from downtown Seattle; I-90 east to Exit 22 ("Preston-Fall City"); go north 3 mi. and bear left at the "Y"; follow signs ½ mi. farther to The Herbfarm.
Hours	March 1 to New Year's eve, every day 9 A.M. to 6 P.M.; January to March, Thursday to Sunday 10 A.M. to 5 P.M.; closed Thanksgiving, Christmas, and New Year's days; restaurant luncheons, mid-March through January, Friday through Sunday; call above number for reservations; weekend snack bar, mid-April through October.
Admission	No fee.
Wheelchair access	Throughout.
Special features	Commercial nursery.

THE RHODODENDRON SPECIES FOUNDATION
P.O. Box 3798   Weyerhaeuser Way   Federal Way, WA 98063-3798
(206) 661-9377 ▪ P ⊻ ⅲ GT ▣ ⏎

Directions	Located at the Weyerhaeuser corporate headquarters in Federal Way; I-5 to exit 142A (Hwy. 18); exit at Weyerhaeuser Way, go north and follow signs to the garden.
Hours	March 1 through October 31, Saturday through Wednesday; November 1 through February 28, Sunday through Wednesday, 11 A.M. to 4 P.M. on all days open; guided tours, March through May, Sunday at 1 P.M., other times by reservation; group tours weekdays by appointment.
Admission	Fee charged; no fee for children age 11 and under.
Wheelchair access	Throughout.
Special features	Bonsai collection.

STATE CAPITOL CONSERVATORY
State Capitol Visitor Services   14th & Capitol AB-12   Olympia, WA 98504
(206) 586-8687 ▪ P ⊻ GT

Directions	Located at 11th and Water Sts., on the West Capitol Campus.
Hours	Grounds, every day, dawn to dusk; conservatory, 8 A.M. to 4:30 P.M., Monday through Friday during winter months and seven days a week from Memorial Day to Labor Day; for information about guided tours of the grounds and the conservatory, call (206) 586-TOUR.
Admission	No fee.
Wheelchair access	Throughout.
Special features	State government complex.

CHILDREN'S HOSPITAL & MEDICAL CENTER
Grounds Maintenance Department   4800 Sand Point Way N.E.   P.O. Box C5371
Seattle, WA 98105
(206) 527-3889 **☐P ⌷ ✗ ⅲ**

Directions	Located in northeast Seattle; take I-5 to Northeast 45th St. exit eastbound; travel 2 mi.; 45th St. becomes Sand Point Way; hospital is on the right.
Hours	Every day, dawn to dusk; for information about the gardens, ask to be directed to the Grounds Maintenance Department.
Admission	No fee.
Wheelchair access	Gardens may be viewed from various points, but direct access is limited because hospital is situated on a hillside.
Special features	Pediatric hospital.

CARL S. ENGLISH, JR., GARDENS
Hiram M. Chittenden Locks   3015 N.W. 54th Street   Seattle, WA 98107
(206) 783-7059 **☐P ⌷ GT ⊘**

Directions	Located on N.W. 54th St. near the intersection of N.W. Market St.; I-5 to N.E. 45th St.; exit west; continue about 6 mi.
Hours	Every day 7 A.M. to 9 P.M.
Admission	No fee.
Wheelchair access	Throughout.
Special features	Chittenden navigational locks, of particular interest to children.

JAPANESE GARDEN OF WASHINGTON PARK ARBORETUM
Seattle Department of Parks and Recreation   Horticulture Section
100 Dexter Avenue North   Seattle, WA 98109
(206) 684-4725 **☐P ⌷ GT ▨**

Directions	Located in the southern tip of Washington Park Arboretum (see below).
Hours	March 1 to November 30, every day from 10 A.M.; closing times vary with season (call for current schedule); guided tours by advance reservation; call 10 A.M. to 4 P.M. weekdays and weekends; "Chado—The Way of Tea" demonstrations in Tea House, third Sunday of every month, 2 and 3 P.M.
Admission	Fee charged; no fee for children age 5 and under.
Wheelchair access	Limited.
Special features	Tea House and Tea-House Garden.

WASHINGTON PARK ARBORETUM
2300 Arboretum Drive East   Seattle, WA 98112
(206) 543-8800 or (206) 543-8616   ∎ P ⚲ ⛴ 👥 GT ⑦ ⏎

Directions	Located off Rte. 520, on the eastern edge of Seattle; from downtown, take Madison St. to Lake Washington Blvd. East; turn left into the arboretum.
Hours	Every day 7 A.M. to dusk; Visitor Center and gift shop, weekdays 10 A.M. to 4 P.M., weekends and holidays noon to 4 P.M.; guided tours every Sunday at 1 P.M.; group tours by advance reservation.
Admission	No fee.
Wheelchair access	Limited.
Special features	Courses offered by the University of Washington Center for Urban Horticulture.

WOODLAND PARK ZOOLOGICAL GARDENS
5500 Phinney Avenue North   Seattle, WA 98103
(206) 684-4800   P ✗ 👥 GT ⑦ ⏎

Directions	Located on Phinney Ave., between North 50th and 59th Sts., near the south shore of Green Lake.
Hours	Zoo, every day, November through February, 10 A.M. to 4 P.M.; March and October, 10 A.M. to 5 P.M.; April through September, weekdays 10 A.M. to 6 P.M., weekends and holidays 8:30 A.M. to 6 P.M.; rose garden, every day, dawn to dusk.
Admission	Fee charged for zoo; no fee for children age 5 and under; no fee for rose garden.
Wheelchair access	Throughout.
Special features	Zoo with 1,000 animals.

MANITO PARK CONSERVATORY AND GARDENS
Spokane Parks Department   4 West 21st Avenue   Spokane, WA 99203
(509) 456-4331   ∎ P ⚲ ⛴ ✗ GT

Directions	Located on Grand Blvd. between 17th and 25th Aves.; Japanese garden is situated on the western edge of the park at the intersection of Bernard St. and 21st Ave.
Hours	Every day 8 A.M. to ½ hour before dusk; Japanese garden closed November 1 through April 15.
Admission	No fee.
Wheelchair access	Throughout.
Special features	Children's playground and wading pool.

POINT DEFIANCE PARK
5402 North Shirley Avenue Tacoma, WA 98407
(206) 591-5328 **P** ⛲⚓**GT**

Directions	I-5 to Bremerton exit west; continue to Pearl St.
Hours	Every day, dawn to dusk; guided tours by advance reservation.
Admission	No fee, except for the camellia garden, requiring admission to the zoo.
Wheelchair access	Throughout.
Special features	Recreational attractions for the whole family, including an aquarium and a zoo.

W. W. SEYMOUR BOTANICAL CONSERVATORY
316 South G Street Tacoma, WA 98405
(206) 591-5330 **P** ⛲**GT**

Directions	Located in Tacoma's Wright Park; from I-5 take Exit 133 to the city's center; follow signs for Rte. 705 north; take Stadium Way exit; right on Stadium Way; left on 4th St.; continue to G St. and the park.
Hours	Every day, September through May, 8:30 A.M. to 4:20 P.M.; June 1 through Labor Day, 8:30 A.M. to 8:00 P.M.; closed Thanksgiving and Christmas days; group tours by advance reservation.
Admission	No fee.
Wheelchair access	Throughout.
Special features	Historic conservatory restoration; Halloween pumpkin festival for children.

OHME GARDENS
3327 Ohme Road Wenatchee, WA 98801
(509) 662-5785 **P**

Directions	Located 3 mi. north of Wenatchee, near the junction of Hwys. 2 and 97.
Hours	Every day, April 15 through October 15; spring (before Memorial Day) 9 A.M. to 6 P.M.; summer 9 A.M. to 7 P.M.; fall (after Labor Day) 9 A.M. to 6 P.M.
Admission	Fee charged; no fee for children age 6 and under.
Wheelchair access	None.

CANADA

BRITISH COLUMBIA

PARK & TILFORD GARDENS

BCE Development Corporation   440-333 Brooksbank Avenue
North Vancouver, BC V7J 3S8
(604) 984-8200 ▣ P ⴲ ⚓

Directions	Located in North Vancouver (20 mins. from downtown) at the Park & Tilford Shopping Centre, intersection of Low Level Rd. and Brooksbank Ave.
Hours	Every day 9:30 A.M. to dusk, with some seasonal variation.
Admission	No fee.
Wheelchair access	Throughout.

FANTASY GARDEN WORLD

10800 No. 5 Road   Richmond, BC V7A 4E5
(604) 271-9325 ▣ P ⴲ ⚓ ✕ ⛪

Directions	Richmond is located 20 mins. south of downtown Vancouver; take Hwy. 99 south to the Steveston Hwy. exit just before the Massey Tunnel.
Hours	Summer months, 9 A.M. to dusk; winter months, 10 A.M. to dusk; 1st week in December through the end of the 1st week in January (Christmas light show), noon to 9 P.M.; light show begins at 4 P.M.; closed Christmas Day.
Admission	Fee charged.
Wheelchair access	Throughout; wheelchairs available at ticket booth.
Special features	Retail garden center with a wide variety of plants for sale; aviaries; children's rides and petting zoo.

RICHMOND NATURE PARK
11851 Westminster Highway and No. 5 Road   Richmond, BC V6X 1B4
(604) 273-7015 ▪ P ⚲ 📷 GT ⑦ 🎦 ↵

Directions	Located about 6 mi. from Vancouver's city center; take Oak St. Bridge to Shell Rd./Richmond center exit; Shell Rd. south to Westminster Hwy.; turn left (east) and continue to first left turn lane into the park.
Hours	Grounds, every day, dawn to dusk; family activities, including guided walks, every weekend during the summer; Nature House, every day 10 A.M. to 4:30 P.M.
Admission	No fee.
Wheelchair access	Throughout.
Special features	Hands-on and live-animal exhibits, of particular delight for children.

MINTER GARDENS
52892 Bunker Road   Rosedale, BC V2P 1X0
(604) 794-7191 ▪ P ⚲ ✕ 📷 GT

Mailing address: Minter Gardens P.O. Box 40   Chilliwack, BC V2P 6H7

Directions	Located about 70 mi. east of Vancouver; take Rte. 1 to the Harrison Hot Springs exit.
Hours	Every day 9 A.M. to dusk, April 1 to October 30.
Admission	Fee charged; no fee for children age 5 and under; extra fee charged for guided tour.
Wheelchair access	Throughout; wheelchairs available at no charge.
Special features	Aviaries; children's petting zoo.

BLOEDEL CONSERVATORY
Vancouver Board of Parks and Recreation   2099 Beach Avenue
Vancouver, BC V6G IZ4
(604) 872-5513 ▪ P ⚲ ✕ 📷 GT

Directions	Located in Queen Elizabeth Park, in downtown Vancouver at the intersection of 33rd Ave. and Cambie St.
Hours	Queen Elizabeth Park, every day, dawn to dusk; Bloedel Conservatory and Civic Arboretum, mid-April to September 30, 10 A.M. to 9 P.M., October 1 to mid-April, 10 A.M. to 5 P.M.
Admission	Fee charged for conservatory; no fee for park.
Wheelchair access	Throughout.
Special features	Planetarium; children's recreational activities.

STANLEY PARK
Vancouver Board of Parks and Recreation   2099 Beach Avenue
Vancouver, BC V6G IZ4
(604) 872-5513   ∎**P**⚐✕

Directions	Located on the north side of Vancouver, at the western end of West Georgia St.
Hours	Every day, 24 hours.
Admission	No fee.
Wheelchair access	Throughout.
Special features	Outdoor summer theater; zoo; aquarium.

DR. SUN YAT-SEN CLASSICAL CHINESE GARDEN
578 Carrall Street   Vancouver, BC V6B 2J8
(604) 689-7133   ∎**P** ⛩ **GT** ⑦ Ⓜ

Directions	Located in the Chinatown section of downtown Vancouver, adjacent to the Dr. Sun Yat-Sen Park and the Chinese Cultural Centre, at the corner of Pender and Carrall Sts.
Hours	Every day, May 1 to September 1, 10 A.M. to 7:30 P.M., September 1 to May 1, 10 A.M. to 4:30 P.M.; guided tours, every day at 10:30 and 11:30 A.M. and on the hour from 1 to 5 P.M. in summer, 1 to 4 P.M. in winter.
Admission	Fee charged.
Wheelchair access	Throughout.
Special features	Chinese Cultural Centre, offering periodic exhibits.

UNIVERSITY OF BRITISH COLUMBIA BOTANICAL GARDEN
6250 Stadium Road   Vancouver, BC V6T 1W5

Mailing address: 6501 N.W. Marine Drive   Vancouver, BC V6T 1W5
(604) 228-4208 ∎ P ⛲ ⅲ GT ⑦ 🖻 ⤶

Directions	UBC campus located at western end of Vancouver; entrance to main garden is at 6250 Stadium Rd., near 16th Ave. and S.W. Marine Dr.; entrance to Nitobe Memorial Garden at 6565 N.W. Marine Dr.
Hours	Every day, March 17 to 31, 10 A.M. to 5 P.M.; April 1 to May 31, 10 A.M. to 7 P.M.; June 1 to August 31, 10 A.M. to 8 P.M.; September 1 to 30, 10 A.M. to 6 P.M.; October 1 to 8, 10 A.M. to 5 P.M.; October 9 to March 15, 10 A.M. to 3 P.M.; Nitobe Garden closed weekends, October 9 to March 15: guided tours, Tuesday and Thursday, by prearrangement (at least 2 weeks); call (604) 731-8982.
Admission	Separate fees for main garden and Nitobe Garden; no fees Wednesday and October 9 to March 15; discount rate for groups of 10 or more.
Wheelchair access	Most areas.
Special features	University campus; garden hot line: (604) 228-5858; plant sale every fall.

VANDUSEN BOTANICAL GARDEN
5251 Oak Street   Vancouver, BC V6M 4H1
(604) 266-7194 ∎ P ⛲ ✕ ⅲ GT ⑦ 🖻 ⤶

Directions	Located at the northwest corner of 37th Ave. and Oak St. in the Shaughnessy district of Vancouver.
Hours	Every day, June through August, 10 A.M. to 9 P.M.; April and September, 10 A.M. to 6 P.M.; May, 10 A.M. to 8 P.M.; October through March, 10 A.M. to 4 P.M.; closed Christmas Day; guided tours, every Sunday at 2 P.M. (3 P.M. during summer); group tours by advance reservation; call Monday through Friday, 9 A.M. to 4 P.M.
Admission	Fee charged; no fee for children age 5 and under.
Wheelchair access	Throughout.
Special features	Original sculptures; totem poles; nature exhibit (MacMillan Bloedel Place); reference library.

THE BUTCHART GARDENS

Benvenuto Road   P.O. Box 4010   Station A   Victoria,BC V8X 3X4
(604) 652-4422   ◼ P ⊥ ✗ ⅲ ⓘ

Directions	Located 15 mi. north of Victoria; Rte. 17 to Butchart-Brentwood exit; left at Keating Rd., 5½ mi. to the garden.
Hours	Opens every day at 9 A.M.; closing times: October, November, January, February, 4 P.M.; March, April, 5 P.M.; December, 8 P.M.; May, June, September, 9 P.M.; July and August, 11 P.M.
Admission	Fee charged; no fee for children age 4 and under.
Wheelchair access	Throughout.
Special features	Estate restoration; musical presentations, animated cartoons for children, and fireworks on summer evenings; gardens are artfully lighted at night, mid-May through September.

FABLE COTTAGE ESTATE

Scenic Marine Drive North   5187 Cordova Bay Road   Victoria, BC V8Y 2K7
(604) 658-5741   ◼ P ✗ ⅲ GT

Directions	Located off Hwy. 17 (Patricia Bay Hwy.) on Scenic Marine Dr., about 20 mins. north of downtown Victoria.
Hours	Every day, mid-March through mid-October, 9:30 A.M. to dusk; guided tours of the cottage interior are continuous throughout the day.
Admission	Fee charged.
Wheelchair access	Throughout.
Special features	Estate restoration; animated figures for children.

HATLEY PARK—ROYAL ROADS MILITARY COLLEGE
F.M.O. Victoria, BC V0S 1B0
(604) 388-1660 ∎ P ⊔ **GT** ⑦

Directions	Located in the 1900 block, Sooke Rd., Colwood area of Victoria.
Hours	Every day 10 A.M. to 4 P.M.; guided tours in summer only.
Admission	No fee.
Wheelchair access	Limited.
Special features	Estate restoration; military college campus.

LIST OF GARDENS

PHOTO CREDITS

All photographs courtesy of the gardens with the exception of those listed below.

INDEX

Page numbers in *italic* indicate illustrations